Dr. Gramma Karen

Helping
Young Parents
and Grandparents
Deal with
Thorny Issues

Dr. Gramma Karen

Helping Young Parents and Grandparents Deal with Thorny Issues

KAREN L. RANCOURT, Ph.D.

Family Links Press
Fort Lauderdale, FL

Ask Dr. Gramma Karen
Helping Young Parents and Grandparents Deal with Thorny Issues

Editorial Production: Diane O'Connell, Write to Sell Your Book, LLC
Cover/Interior Design: Susan Newman Design, Inc.
Author Photo: Jan Logozzo

Publisher's Note: This book is designed to provide accurate information in regard to the subject matter covered. It is sold with the understanding that the publisher and author are not engaged in rendering psychological, financial, legal, or other professional services. If expert assistance or counseling is needed, the reader should seek the services of a competent professional. This book contains website urls that may eventually no longer be live.

To contact the author, e-mail Karen@mommybites.com.

Printed in the United States of American for Worldwide Distribution
ISBN: 978-0-9896274-0-5

Also by
Karen L. Rancourt, Ph.D.

Yeah But, Children Need... (1978)

The Empowered Professional:
How to be Successful in the 1990s (1990)

Empowered Professionals: Making a Difference (1992)

For my grandchildren,
all the kids who call me Gramma Karen,
and children everywhere.
It's all about you.

{CONTENTS}

{INTRODUCTION}

I remember the exact moment I became interested in the relationships between young parents and their parents, between young parents and their in-laws. I was sitting poolside keeping an eye on my then-three-year-old grandson while chatting with another grandmother who was watching her grandchild. She asked me if I had a place at the beach community on the Jersey Shore where this conversation was taking place.

I explained that my husband and I were living with our daughter, son-in-law, and two grandsons in their vacation home for the summer. As the other grandmother was saying how nice that must be for us, she was cut off mid-sentence by a young woman seated two lounge chairs away, who yelled over to us with undisguised hostility, "You couldn't build a house big enough for me to live with my parents or in-laws!" Whoa! Where did that come from?

As a result of this young mom's negative comment about her relationships with her parents and in-laws, I began researching parent-grandparent relationships to understand better why some are solid, loving, and fulfilling while others are uncomfortable, unpleasant, and sometimes contentious. I used this research for a presentation I called "Oh, _____! My Mother/Mother-in-Law is Coming." The responses used to fill in the blank ranged from "Fantastic!" to . . . well, use your imagination. My audiences, primarily young moms, and often their moms and their mothers-in-law, were enthusiastic, had a lot to say, and were very interested in what advice I had to offer.

Based on the success of these presentations, I decided to expand my audience by writing an advice column for young parents and grandparents. Although other personal advice columns exist, there did not seem to be one spotlighting the unique issues that impact young parents, grandparents, and grandchildren. On a personal level I was excited about writing this column for several reasons. At my post-60 age (okay, pre-70 age), I am less focused on my career and more interested in spending time with family and friends; running, biking, kayaking with my husband; wave running with my grandsons.

Writing an advice column would allow me to be professionally engaged while drawing on my skills and talents in a fun way, but most important, it would let me help parents and grandparents build and sustain the family relationships they'd like to have, or have and want to maintain. I won't bore you with the details of my background and endeavors except to say I am a wife, mother, grandmother, author, educator, corporate consultant, and career and parenting coach—lots of varied and wonderful experience to draw upon.

Obviously I needed a platform to publish my advice column, and so, for two reasons, I decided to approach Mommybites (www.mommybites.com), a Manhattan-based, national online community for parenting resources, support, education, tele-classes, webinars, videos, and blogs.

First, Mommybites had announced plans to include a new offering focused on family, and I figured my column would be a timely and relevant addition. Second, since my daughter Heather is a Mommybites co-owner, I thought my idea might be seriously considered. Happily for me, and I trusted for my potential readers, they agreed to my writing a column. (Guilty: shameless nepotism.)

So, Mommybites introduced me to their community in

September 2011, and *Ask Dr. Gramma Karen: An Advice Column for Young Parents and Grandparents* went live. I invited readers to submit to me difficult situations involving parents and grandparents for which they would like my advice. I, in turn, would select situations that I thought would have broad appeal to other parents and grandparents. Much to my delight, my column was well received and has garnered a strong and growing following. Several readers suggested I compile my columns into a book, a suggestion I took to heart.

A word about how I have organized *Ask Dr. Gramma Karen: Helping Young Parents and Grandparents Deal with Thorny Issues*. Each chapter is stand-alone, meaning the chapters are not interdependent and do not have to be read sequentially. However, to make navigating the chapters easier, I have grouped the chapters into five parts.

"Part One, Involvement: The Need for Boundaries" deals with difficult issues young parents face when they feel the grandparents are too involved in the parenting of their grandchildren. Then there are the young parents who wish the grandparents were more involved in their grandchildren's lives. Grandparents also raise issues about when it is appropriate or inappropriate for them to get involved in the parenting of their grandchildren. The topic of how to set and implement boundaries is essential in this section, with do's and don'ts for both young moms and grandmothers.

"Part Two, Communication: The Need to Get It Right" offers perspectives on the full range of potential missteps— communication that is ineffective, lacking, inaccurate, or difficult. As evident in a couple of the situations, guilt is often a natural by-product of poor communication.

"Part Three, Assumptions and Expectations: Avoiding Disappointment" presents situations parents and grandparents face that at first glance may seem to have obvious solutions, but when subjected to further analysis, it becomes apparent that things are not always as they seem. We often discover that much of the underlying stress and contention exists because the people involved have made erroneous assumptions or have set their hearts on certain things happening based on misinformation or misunderstandings.

"Part Four, Power and Control: Letting Go of the Need to Win" addresses parent-grandparent-grandchildren issues in which being or vying to be the alpha male/female trumps all other considerations. Often people do not realize they are caught up in various kinds of relationship competitions, and those in the running often include grandchildren who are trying to assert themselves over their parents and grandparents. Helping family members shift from a win-lose model to one of collaboration and cooperation can make all the difference.

"Part Five, Values, Beliefs and Principles: The Need to Consider Accommodation" requires parents, grandparents, and grandchildren to consider putting their own needs on the back burner in order to preserve or enhance family relationships. When values and beliefs are the root causes of family problems, the challenge becomes one of moving from a right-wrong mode of thinking to one where the goal is to acknowledge differences and to focus on how to make sure those differences do not become permanent, detrimental wedges in the relationships.

In short, a reader can simply look at the Contents and read the parts or chapters in any order, based on interest. In addition to my response to a reader's specific issue, often there is a section of readers' responses to the issue, as well as inclusion of other articles I have written about the topic at hand. To protect the confidentiality and anonymity of those submitting situations, I changed some of the details.

I know my columns are timely and relevant because the issues are submitted by young parents and grandparents. They regularly read my columns, they say, because they appreciate that my advice applies to numerous interpersonal situations and is not limited to relationships between young parents and grandparents. This is my intent: I don't tell people what to do, but rather, I try to present a range of options and alternatives and discuss the pros and cons of each, leaving it to the person who submitted the situation to decide which option is best suited for his/her personality and circumstances. Readers tell me that I typically present for each issue a suggestion or two they had not considered.

This feedback pleases me! Yes, my primary focus is on strengthening relationships between young parents and grandparents, with grandchildren being the ultimate benefactors, but so much the better if my advice applies to other relationships, too. I hope I "de-thorn" thorny issues so they seem less complicated, perplexing and overwhelming, thus helping everyone, especially young parents and grandparents, build more respectful, sustainable, and enjoyable relationships.

PART 1

Involvement
The Need for Boundaries

{Chapter 1}

My Daughter-in-Law Told Me I Was Interfering with Her Parenting

Dear Dr. Gramma Karen:

When does giving advice become interfering? I ask because my daughter-in-law told me that I was "interfering with her parenting" when I told her she should let my granddaughter go to a sleepover birthday party. My granddaughter is 12 and tends to be a bit shy. I think this party would be a great opportunity for her to build some good friendships.

My feelings were hurt and when I tried to talk with my son about it he said I needed to talk with my daughter-in-law. I don't know if I should just let this go or if I should explain to my daughter-in-law why I gave the advice that I did. I thought we had a good relationship and this has really upset me.

You ask, "When does giving advice become interfering?" I don't mean for this to sound flip, but the simple answer is: Whenever your daughter-in-law says you're interfering. Yes, you have good intentions, and yes, you are thinking about your granddaughter, and yes, you have lots of experience to bring to the table, but none of this matters. What does matter at this point is that your daughter-in-law has told you that you interfered with her parenting.

Your situation reminds me of a classic scene in the 1989 Batman movie where the Alicia Hunt character (played by Jerry Mack) and Jack Nicholson, who plays Jack Napier, the Joker, are standing in front of a mirror. Unsolicited, Hunt compliments Napier by saying in a sultry voice, "You look fine." Napier/Nicholson drawls in reply, "I didn't ask."

And there it is in a nutshell: "I didn't ask." Napier/Nicholson didn't ask. Your daughter-in-law didn't ask.

I think talking with your daughter-in-law is in order, but I suggest you not start the conversation by explaining (in effect, justifying) why you said you think your granddaughter should be allowed to attend the sleepover. If you start the conversation this way, you will be telling her in a polite way that what you said was appropriate and that she is incorrect in thinking you were interfering. She has already said you were interfering, so let's start there. To set the right tone, your might begin by saying: "I owe you an apology for interfering in the situation about Darlene's (fictitious name) invitation to the sleepover. You didn't ask for my opinion. I am really sorry." And then stop talking.

There are a variety of responses you may get from your daughter-in-law, e.g., "I was not really upset about what you said. I am upset because I heard from a neighbor that the girl's family giving the sleepover has a huge dog that bites." Or, "I know you meant well, but saying that in front of Darlene made me the bad guy and you the good guy." Or, "You've been doing this more and more, and I've wanted to talk to you about it." Or, "Apology accepted. No big deal."

Whatever the response, you'll have a better idea of where you are in your relationship with your daughter-in-law, and you'll know what you need to say. What happened between the two of you could be a minor one-off, or it could be an indication of something that needs to be addressed. It does, however, raise the issue of giving unsolicited advice. (And yes, there are those rare times involving health and safety, when unsolicited advice must be given. For example, you hear from the local librarian that the sleepover is not going to be chaperoned and kids all over town know about it and plan on crashing it. This is surely a time to speak up.)

In the future, whenever you find yourself wanting to give your daughter-in-law unsolicited advice, it is worth envisioning Jack Nicholson saying, "I didn't ask." Remembering these three words can help you decide if giving your advice might very well be interfering with her parenting.

Side comment: I applaud your son for telling you to take up your hurt directly with your daughter-in-law. He, in effect, is giving you some good advice—solicited advice that you asked for when you approached him—by letting you know he doesn't want to be in the middle of the situation between you and your daughter-in-law. Good for him! There are times when a son or daughter needs to protect their spouse from a parent or in-law, but this is not one of those times.

(Note: To watch the "I didn't ask" scene with Nicholson, go to http://www.imdb.com/video/screenplay/vi850985241/ and after the short ad, go to the 50th second of the clip.)

{Readers' Comments}

Dear Readers:

This column, "My Daughter-in-Law Told Me I Was Interfering with Her Parenting," generated a lot of emotional e-mails I want to share, as well as include my additional comments.

One grandfather wrote: *"I do not like the image of 'walking on egg shells' when considering when an in-law can give unsolicited advice. However, it raises a question: Does your advice also apply to the parents of grown children, or, in fact, to any relationship?"*

You raise a good point about the extent to which my advice might apply to other relationships. My advice is general and each person has to think about it within the context of his/her own situations and relationships. Yes, it might apply to the parents of grown children—again, depending on the relationships. Some grown children welcome their parents' advice, others tolerate it, some resent it, and for others it is a combination, depending on the situation. Maybe some grandparents are needlessly "walking on egg shells," whereas others should be! The only way to know for sure is to discuss it, and I hope my columns expedite such discussions.

For example, a grandmother wrote: *"My husband and I were discussing your column on giving advice at dinner last night. We were saying how it took just that one word of 'interfering' to cause the upset. I think that communication is such risky business with every relationship. One never knows whether whatever one says to another person is received in the manner in which it was intended. And timing is of great importance, too. In fact, I have found myself in that situation with my daughter on several occasions. When we talk it over, it most often is that I have reacted without all the information I needed."*

You make an excellent point about the advice giver's intentions often causing problems and having unintended impacts on the one receiving the advice. That's why well-intentioned help is often experienced as "interference," i.e., meddling, judging, and worst of all, criticizing. Anytime we say "you should . . . ," it is difficult not to interpret this as, "If you were as smart as I am, you would know to do such and such." Of course this is not the hoped-for impact, but, many times, there you are.

However, there are ways we can minimize the risk that our giving advice will cause problems by using some simple communication that tests the waters before we dive in. For example, if we're involved in a situation in which we want to give input and/or solutions, we can say, "Would it be helpful if I gave you my opinion/advice?" And then we need to listen carefully to the answer and pay attention to the body language. Sighs of exasperation, eyes rolling heavenward, and arms crossed across the chest say a lot.

And, yes, timing is critical, too. Sometimes we can increase our chances of being listened to if some time has passed and elevated emotions have a chance to abate. Then we might begin by saying, "I've been thinking about that situation from yesterday, and if it would be helpful, I have some advice for you to consider." Again, the emphasis is on positioning yourself as wanting to be helpful, not intrusive or interfering, and the best way to do this is to say explicitly, "I am trying to be helpful . . . " Then we have to be prepared for being told that we are, in fact, not being helpful. Also, even if the advice is welcomed, it does not guarantee it will be followed, and it does not mean that any future, unsolicited advice will be gladly received.

Another grandmother wrote: *"My situation is a bit different. When I was a young mother, both my mother and mother-in-law gave me so much advice my head spun. I vowed that when I was a grandmother I was not going to give advice. And that is what I did for months after my first grandchild was born. Even when asked for my advice, I would backpedal and say nothing, or something like, 'Whatever you do will be good.'*

"My daughter finally sat me down and said, 'Mom, when I ask for your advice, it's because I need it. When you clam up it feels like you don't care.' Now when I have some advice, I give my daughter this certain look, tilt my head to the right, and she says, 'Okay. Tell

me.' And I do."

This grandmother's comment is a good reminder that the rules and boundaries for giving advice in any relationship will vary, but one constant is the value of having some discussion about the circumstances under which receiving advice is helpful and when it is not. Most young parents will probably feel comfortable initiating this conversation with their own parents, but in many cases, the grandparents may have to take the lead.

{Chapter 2}

I Dread Thanksgiving Dinner with My Husband's Family

Dear Dr. Gramma Karen:

I am dreading the annual Thanksgiving dinner with my husband's family. My father-in-law (FIL) and his brother have strong and differing political opinions and they will inevitably end up having one of their shouting matches. It is so upsetting to me, and I envision our three-year-old son James being aware of it this year and also getting upset. James gets anxious when my husband and I raise our voices with each other.

When my FIL and his brother start going at it, the other members of the family (there are 15 of us, including four cousins) roll their eyes at each other in a kind of here-we-go-again way, but no one tries to stop it. It just keeps escalating until one of them stomps off in anger. Then everyone pretends it never happened.

Aside from this, I really do look forward to being with everyone, especially for James's sake. His cousins are older and they make a big fuss over him. I want James to have these family connections, so dropping out of the Thanksgiving dinner isn't something I really want to do. Other than this exchange with his brother, my father-in-law is a real sweetheart, as is my mother-in-law (MIL). My husband finds the yelling match upsetting, too, but he doesn't think it's worth trying to stop it; he says they've always done this. I am not sure I have any other options than to just put up with it.

I think your first sentence would be more accurate if it read: "I enjoy having Thanksgiving dinner with my husband's family, with the exception of my father-in-law and his brother's annual ritual of having arguments about politics." It is the anticipation of and the actual shouting match that stress you out, so it might be helpful to hone in on them and consider some options.

First, what are some things you might do before the Thanksgiving dinner? Appealing to the "sweetheart" aspects of your father-in-law's personality could prove fruitful. For example, you and your husband might get on the phone with both your FIL and MIL and explain that you need their help because of late you've noticed James gets agitated and upset when he's around raised, angry voices.

You can explain that knowing Gramps and Uncle Joe typically have a passionate and emotional exchange about politics with raised voices, you are hoping they will help you out and take the discussion outside, away from everyone, and not have it at the dinner table. Further, you can explain that you'd appreciate Gramps calling Uncle Joe before Thanksgiving Day and getting his agreement to take it outside.

I think it is important to have your MIL part of this conversation because her knowing about your request makes it more difficult for your FIL to ignore or downplay your request. It is possible she's talked with your FIL in private about this disruptive exchange he has with his brother; she may feel she's been fighting a lonely battle and is glad you're bringing it up.

You may notice that I'm suggesting you ask your FIL and his brother to take the unpleasant exchange outside, that is, you're not asking them to stop the exchange all together, even though that would be the more mature and ideal thing for them to do. Your request is merely asking them to change their venue, not their behavior, as asking them to change their behavior could make them just dig in more. You just need them to do their thing out of earshot. If they agree, problem solved.

However, if you don't get the cooperation you're looking for, you need to have a backup plan. Here is one that's simple and straightforward: If the exchange begins at the dinner table, you and your husband take James, excuse yourselves, and ask someone to call you when Gramps and Uncle Joe have finished their argument. Your explanation is that you find the raised voices and the arguing stressful and you'd rather not be around it, especially for James's sake. You can go to another part of the house, take a walk, go for a ride—you may even find other family members joining you! Your FIL, your MIL, and Uncle Joe, assuming he's been called, won't be surprised at your leaving because you would have told them in the pre-Thanksgiving dinner phone call that this is your plan.

Based on your description of the situation, my advice is predicated on the assumption that your FIL's and Uncle Joe's arguments are loud and heated, but do not include profanity and/ or racial, gender or ethnic disparagements of any kind. If any of these have been part of the previous arguments, I think you are completely justified in having a different pre-Thanksgiving phone call, one in which you're not asking them to merely take the exchange outside, but one in which you inform them that you need their commitment not to talk about anything that riles one or both of them, because you do not want your son to witness any of the offensive, unacceptable, and embarrassing behavior that his grandfather demonstrates. This would definitely be a situation calling for unequivocal tough love from the parents to a grandparent.

Initiating some pre-event communication to try to get some behavioral commitments in advance may prove helpful. Further, because you are clear on what you intend to do if these commitments are not given or not honored, this will hopefully motivate your FIL and his brother to behave appropriately so everyone at the Thanksgiving dinner table can relax and enjoy being together.

{Readers' Comments}

Dear Readers:

Preparing for Thanksgiving and hosting the day can be stressful, yet it can be difficult to give up, modify or change traditions. Many thanks to you, my readers, for sharing some of the things you have stopped doing and/or have started doing to reduce your Thanksgiving holiday stress. Others may benefit from your suggestions. Good food for thought!

No More Trying to Accommodate Dietary Requirements and Preferences

"I have stopped trying to accommodate my mother-in-law's numerous dietary requirements and preferences—all of which were taking the fun out of my Thanksgiving preparations. For example, garlic and onions make her burp, she doesn't like chestnuts in her dressing, and she prefers roast pork to turkey. As politely as I could, I asked her to please bring her own dinner this year.

"When she seemed a bit insulted about it, I told her that by bringing her own food we could both be assured that everything she ate would be acceptable to her. I reminded her that when it's just a small gathering I try to plan around her, but for a large Thanksgiving dinner full of traditional dishes, many of which are prepared by others, I am not easily able to do so. My husband totally supports me in this and told his mother so."

I Have Decreed There Will Be No Electronic Devices

"This year Thanksgiving in my home is to be digital-free: no i anythings will be allowed. I am tired of my family working their keyboards and not interacting with each other. My daughter, one of the worst offenders, said, "You've got to be kidding!" I assured her I am serious. I have asked my grandchildren to bring board games and other non-digital activities they can do together. My family may not like it, but they can all send me an e-mail or text after Thanksgiving to complain. My house, my rules."

I've Put the Grandchildren to Work

"I have four grandchildren under the age of ten coming to my house for Thanksgiving. Last year I set up a table for them on which I had light cardboard cut into place-mat size, crayons, magic markers, and stickers. Instead of running around they worked on making place mats for everyone. They enjoyed being with each and working on the project together and they asked to do it again this year."

I Will Not Be Bringing My Mother from Assisted Living

"My mother lives nearby in assisted living. For the first time I am not bringing her to my home for Thanksgiving. There are about 30 of us and it is noisy and confusing for her, and after about 20 minutes or so, she wants to go home. Getting her here, worrying about her, and her wanting to leave after a few minutes is nothing but stressful for me. "This year I will visit with her early on Thanksgiving morning and my sister will visit her later in the day. The staff where she lives assures me that my new plan is better because my mother always returns from a big family gathering agitated and confused. I feel guilty about this, but I realize having her with the whole family is more about my needs than hers."

Assign Everyone a Task

"This grandmother (me!) just doesn't have the energy I used to have (I am 78), so last year instead of my doing everything for Thanksgiving dinner as I have done in the past, I made a list of every task required, e.g., set the table, get the beverage table ready, distribute the hors d'oeuvres, plate the turkey and all the trimmings, clear the dirty dishes, set out the desserts, wrap the leftovers, clean the kitchen, empty the trash, etc. etc.

"A couple of weeks before Thanksgiving I let everyone know by e-mail their assignment, including the grandchildren. Everyone knew each other's assignment, so there was some trading of tasks—mostly because some family members did not want their task to interfere with the football games on TV.

"It worked well and we're doing it again this year. I think having everyone responsible for some task makes them more aware of what it takes to bring the family together. The Thanksgiving Day feast is a labor of love, but it still is labor!"

Changing How Traditional Dishes are Prepared

"Our Thanksgiving dinner would not be complete without mashed potatoes. My mother and our Italian aunts (all now deceased) would have a fit over this break with tradition, but it saves so much time and it is actually more nutritious. I now use red potatoes; I cut *them into smaller pieces, leave the skins on, and add several garlic cloves to the water. When the potatoes are tender I just use a masher with milk (I heat milk in the microwave so the potatoes don't cool), add butter, salt, pepper, and chives to taste until I get the consistency I want.*

"This way skips all of that baloney with an electric mixer, which is just more bowls and stuff to clean. The little remaining lumps let my guests know that I've used real potatoes. Gone are the days of all that ridiculous peeling. When you're talking 15 plus pounds, that's no small potatoes!"

Starting a Totally New Way to Spend Thanksgiving Day

"I am completely breaking with our usual Thanksgiving schedule this year. Between my grown and married children rushing around trying to spend part of the day with their in-laws and their relatives, and my trying to work around the grandchildren's naps, it was becoming a scheduling nightmare for me.

"This year my husband and I are going to a restaurant around noon for our dinner and anyone can join us who wants to. Then, I am having an "open house" through the early evening. Everyone can come and go according to their other commitments. I will provide snacks, fixings for turkey sandwiches, and desserts. My family understands why I am doing this and they are willing to give it a try. I already feel so relieved!"

Chapter 3

My Daughter-in-Law Excludes
My Husband and Me

Dear Dr. Gramma Karen:

My husband and I raised two children, a daughter and a son. We worked hard while our children were growing up and we were able to put both through good private colleges. In addition, we put our son Derrick through medical school. While at medical school he met Lannie, who is also a practicing physician. Lannie and Derrick have now been married for 15 years. They started their family seven years ago and have three adorable children.

From day one, Lannie has been very cool to my husband and me, always all business, never bothering with any social niceties, like asking how we are. They live five minutes from us, yet the only time they contact us is when they want us to babysit the grandchildren, which we happily do. When Lannie's parents are in town, we are never invited to visit. When Lannie and Derrick host holidays and parties, we are never invited. When I interact with Lannie, it's always about instructions regarding the children while we babysit.

I kept hoping she would warm up towards us, but that has not happened. I find I am getting more and more upset about how cold she is to us. I think I should talk to my son about what's going on and tell him how hurt we feel about the way Lannie treats us. My husband says not to do anything because we do get to spend time with the grandchildren and that is what's really important. What do you think?

Let's start with your statement that "I think I should talk to my son about what's going on . . . " I am struggling to find a kind way to tell you that your son already knows what's been going on—he's known for 15 years that you and your husband have not been invited to holiday and other family gatherings. I also struggle to find gentle words to tell you that obviously your son has apparently decided not to do anything about it. Finally, I have to point out that you are giving your son a free pass by making Lannie the problem, but he's as much a part of your being excluded as is his wife.

If you decide you want to raise this issue, I suggest you and your husband talk with your son and Lannie together. Rather than having a conversation about how hurt you feel about being left out—a conversation that would have made better sense 15 years ago the first time it happened—I suggest you say something specific and proactive: "Looking ahead to the up-and-coming holidays, we'd like to be included. We're happy to host, or if you'd rather host, we'll do whatever you need us to do to help. We hope our being included will be okay with you." This statement is direct, clear, and unemotional: We want to be included. It also lays a foundation for one of three general responses from your son and Lannie.

Lannie and your son may be gracious and simply say that of course it would be wonderful to have you be part of the festivities. It is possible they say they assumed, based on something you said or did many years ago, that you didn't like to attend these kinds of gatherings. They may feel you and your husband have been the ones who preferred to be excluded.

The worst case would be if they were direct and honest with you and said they'd rather you didn't come, because, and I'm making these up by way of examples, "You dominate the conversations," or "You initiate heated controversial discussions," or "You once insulted Lannie's parents," or "You're bossy and opinionated." Ouch. Without becoming defensive, once you get over the shock of learning something negative about yourself, you may want to agree to stop the offensive behavior.

Another possible response is that they make up some lame excuse about why it would be better if you didn't come, e.g., "There are going to be so many people coming and you get to see the grandchildren all the time." This would be code for the fact that they don't want you to come and they don't want to get into the real reasons. If this is the response you get, you're right back where you started, except you would know for sure that you have been deliberately excluded in the past and can expect to be excluded in the future.

At this point you can decide if you want to push for details, but the conversation could become awkward and uncomfortable. After all, you've accepted the situation for 15 years, so your son and Lannie may understandably be puzzled why you're just now getting around to mentioning that you're hurt that you've been excluded. They may shake their heads, thinking the shelf life on this has long expired. I'm trying to prepare you for the possibility that they don't show any concern or empathy.

I have to agree with your husband when he urges you "not to do anything because we do get to spend time with the grandchildren and that is what's really important." So, your best tactic may be to casually ask to be included in family gatherings, and hope your daughter-in-law and son agree, but I suggest you do not push for details and explanations about why you've been excluded for these many years, as this could jeopardize your current access to your grandchildren. In this situation you may want to do as Chaucer suggested in *Troilus and Criseyde* way back in 1380, "It is nought good a slepyng hound to wake." Let sleeping dogs lie.

Chapter 4

I See a Potential Speech Problem, But My Grandson's Parents Don't Agree

Dear Dr. Gramma Karen:

I visit with my son, his wife, and their three-year-old son for a couple of days every six weeks or so. I love spending time with my grandson Michael. My relationship with my son is good. My relationship with my daughter-in-law is okay, but she tends to get snippy with me when I ask even casual questions about how Michael is doing. I really try not to be critical or judgmental, but the conversation seems strained whenever we talk about my grandson. My son tends to ignore these uncomfortable exchanges when he's around us.

Here's where I need some advice. I think Michael may need some help with his speech, as only about half of what he says is understandable. When I mentioned to my son and daughter-in-law that I was having difficulty understanding Michael, they both became very defensive and said their pediatrician said Michael was fine and he would outgrow it. The message I got was: MYOB (Mind Your Own Business).

I talked with the daughter of a friend of mine, a speech and language pathologist, and she said Michael might have some form of a condition that impedes proper speech, something having to do with the muscles of the face and tongue. This is not a condition that a child simply outgrows. She also said that Michael should be given an assessment as soon as possible, because if he has a problem and is not treated, he could lose his self-confidence, become self-conscious, come to dislike school, and avoid social activities when he gets older. I am not sure how to proceed.

You're showing a lot of courage in wanting to proceed. I say this because your situation is one where your goal of wanting your son and daughter-in-law to at least hear what you have to say could have some negative relationship ramifications, as it sounds like your relationship with your daughter-in-law is a bit shaky. If you do become a persona non grata after speaking your mind, hopefully it will be only temporary, but this is a risk perhaps well worth taking if you can help Michael.

If you're of a full-steam-ahead mindset, your immediate challenge is to be clear about what you want to say and how you want to communicate it.

First, what do you want to say? Perhaps you want to make these points:

- You're still having trouble understanding Michael's speech.
- Your only motivation in raising this topic is your love for Michael. You think they're great parents and you are in no way casting aspersions on their parenting.
- Because you're concerned, you've talked with a speech and language pathologist, who said:
  - Speech impediments are common in young children.
  - Many speech difficulties do not self correct.

- An assessment by a trained professional can pinpoint any problems and determine if treatment is warranted, or if the child will outgrow it.
- Treatment, sooner rather than later (before entering school), is best for the child.
- If the treatment required is delayed, the school will eventually pick it up anyway, and the child will have lost valuable treatment time.
- Unaddressed speech problems can make a child a target of teasing; this in turn can result in the child's loss of self-confidence.
- The assessment process is totally benign and does not cause a child any stress or discomfort.
- Some cities and towns pay for speech therapy.
- You got an estimate for the cost of an assessment by a speech therapist, and you would like to pay for this as a gift.
- You hope they agree with you that there is no downside to having Michael assessed; if Michael needs speech therapy, it is good to know now and begin helping him. If Michael doesn't need it, everyone has peace of mind.

Once you're clear on the points you want to make, you need to decide how to deliver your message. I think this is a message that you need to deliver in person, if possible, so that if there is any MYOB behavior from your son, daughter-in-law, or both, you can help lower the emotional pitch by saying over and over, in a calm voice, "Of course the final decision is yours to make. Please just hear me out."

In this way you're reminding them that you just want them to listen to what you have to say, you're trying to influence them with information provided by an expert, and that you know they have the final say.

Your son and daughter-in-law may initially be angry and upset with you, so you must be willing to take this relationship hit. However, my hope is that you are pleasantly surprised by their reaction; that is, they thank you for your concern and the positive steps you've taken on Michael's behalf. Further, I hope they take you up on your generous offer to get an assessment done as soon as possible.

It is possible that they, too, have similar concerns about Michael's speech, but they are reluctant to raise questions because they want to believe the pediatrician's opinion that Michael will outgrow it and/or they are uncomfortable challenging the pediatrician. The suggestions from an expert, the speech and language pathologist with whom you consulted, may be enough to help them to reconsider their position and to stay focused on what is best for Michael.

{Chapter 5}

I Am Afraid Our Baby's Grandmothers Will Be Too Involved

Dear Dr. Gramma Karen:

I am a first-time expectant mom and I can already anticipate very, very involved grandmothers, both of whom live nearby, both of whom have strong opinions about childrearing. I envision both grandmothers constantly telling me what they think I should do. I'd like to set some boundaries for my baby's grandmothers, but I am not sure how to do this.

You've hit on a real phenomenon. If you Google "helicopter parents" (defined as parents who hover over their children and are overly involved in their lives) you'll get approximately 248,000 results. Google "helicopter grandparents" and you'll get somewhere around 2,130,000 results, about a one-to-nine ratio. It seems there's a whole lot going on with helicopter grandparenting!

With their close proximity and strong opinions about how you should raise your child, it is to everyone's benefit if you set some basic ground rules for your mom and mother-in-law (MIL) before the baby comes. To help both expectant/new/young parents and the grandparents have comfortable and productive discussions about expectations and boundaries, I've developed two sets of guidelines—Do's and Don'ts for Grandmothers, and Do's and Don'ts for Young Moms.

These guidelines are suggestions to help you articulate your expectations and to provide a format for sharing them. You may agree with some of the guidelines, disagree with others, or you may want to modify or add to them. I urge you to personalize them so they can help you set boundaries, manage expectations, and have relaxed relationships between your immediate family and the grandmothers.

I summarize my advice to grandparents in this way: "When in doubt, zip it!" It can be difficult to accept, but you're not in the driver's seat anymore: Your children and their spouses are the primary drivers. You are an invited passenger for the most part, so when you are tempted to help with or take over the driving, zip it! This may mean you have to do a lot of biting your tongue.

I summarize my advice for you and all young moms interacting with the grandparents in this way: "Lighten up!" Do not treat every interaction the grandparents have with your baby, or any slight deviations they make regarding your rules, as life threatening. They're not! Lighten up means to keep things in perspective.

Section One:
Do's and Don'ts for Grandmothers

1. Remember that you are a grandparent, not the parent. This means you must do a lot of tongue biting and allow your daughter or daughter-in-law to set the boundaries and rules for your interactions with your grandchildren. If

you want to have ongoing and welcomed access to your grandchildren, Zip it! Zip it! Zip it!

2. Do not try to impose your values or parenting preferences on your daughter or daughter-in-law. Ask her to tell you about any books she'd like you to read or videos to watch that can help you better understand how she's trying to raise her children. Your job is to understand her intended parenting and not try to change it.

3. Pay special attention to your daughter or daughter-in-law's verbal and nonverbal cues. If you sense your behavior is causing her stress or discomfort, reread guideline #1. Also, a sincere apology can go a long way.

4. If you feel your daughter or daughter-in-law prefers to spend more time with the other set of grandparents, you may want to ask if there are any specific things you could do to be a better grandparent. If you ask, your job is to listen, not try to defend or explain yourself.

5. Be very clear on your daughter's or daughter-in-law's preferences about visiting: Should you call first or is showing up unannounced permissible?

6. If you live within commuting distance, talk with your daughter or daughter-in-law about setting aside regular time(s) each week to come into her home. Also discuss how best to use this dedicated time. Knowing she has a free block of time to look forward to every week can make your daughter or daughter-in-law feel like she's won the lottery!

7. If your daughter or daughter-in-law has a nanny or babysitter, discuss with her your role when you're alone with the nanny or babysitter.

8. When you look around your daughter's or daughter-in-

law's house and see some jobs that might be done, ask if it would be helpful if you either did them yourself or hired someone to do them. Over time you will work out with her what things you can automatically do without imposing or causing an issue.

9. Check with your daughter or daughter-in-law before making any purchases of equipment (e.g., car seats, cribs, pack 'n plays, strollers) to keep in your car or house or to be given as gifts.

10. Check with your daughter or daughter-in-law on the appropriateness and timing of all gifts or money.

11. Do not ask your grandchild to be complicit in any secrets. You can plan a surprise with your grandchild, but never ask him/her "to keep this a secret from your parents." Rather, say, "Let's not talk about this surprise with your parents until it's time for the surprise to happen."

12. Support your grown children who are now young parents when they want to carve out their own family traditions, e.g., holidays, birthdays, instead of trying to get them to continue the traditions you've established.

13. Say only positive things about your grandchildren's parents; same goes for any other (step) grandparents and relatives in the family.

14. Do not play favorites amongst your grandchildren; do not make comparisons.

15. If you are a long-distance grandmother, work closely with your daughter or daughter-in-law to make this work for everyone.

   • Take advantage of the Internet, especially with older grandchildren: e.g., e-mail, Skype, share photos and sites with information of places to visit together, share favorite music.

- Keep notes of what you learn from your grandchildren in phone calls or Skyping or visits so you can reference this information in future interactions, e.g., dolls' names, their friends' names, games they like, movies they want to see. This helps the long-distance bonding and is proof positive to your grandchildren that you are listening to them and you are interested in their lives.
- Plan things together to do the next time you'll be together.
- Tell your grandchildren about your hobbies, and when possible, share your hobbies and teach them, e.g., chess, biking, knitting, baking, sailing.

16. When in doubt, zip it!

Section Two:
Do's and Don'ts for Young Moms

1. If there are differences between your parenting practices and those of your mom or mother-in-law (MIL), explain your views, but don't try to get her to agree that you are right. Your mom or MIL merely has to agree to abide by your rules when she interacts with your children.

2. Help your mom or MIL understand your parenting preferences and practices by inviting her to: read the books and view the videos that have influenced you; visit the Web sites and blogs you go to for advice; go together to hear various speakers; listen to the same Webinars on parenting and grandparenting.

3. Do lighten up! Get in touch with what's really going on if you

totally freak out when your mom or MIL lets your child have an extra dessert. It is probably not really about a chocolate chip cookie. You need to figure out what's really bothering you, why it's bothering you, communicate it constructively, and if necessary, make appropriate apologies.

4. Your mom or MIL may have some different rules and boundaries for the grandchildren in her own home. You don't let them jump on the beds in your house, but Grandma doesn't care. You would never let your kids have leftover pizza for breakfast, but Grandma would. However, most rules for routines, such as naps and bedtimes for the younger grandchildren, need to be followed.

5. Be aware of and sensitive to the rivalry or jealousy that can develop between your mom and your MIL, that is, one feeling the other gets special treatment. You may have to lay out some consistent rules you need both your mom and MIL to follow, for example, limits on how much can be spent on gifts.

6. Accept that sometimes you may favor your mom over your MIL, or vice versa. It can be a case of proximity, with one simply living closer than the other and therefore able to be more involved. But sometimes you may prefer the values and/or personality of your mom or MIL. You may simply feel more comfortable around one over the other. Your goal is to use acceptance, kindness, and respect to build the best relationship possible with both your mom and mother-in-law.

7. If you choose to address an issue in a family meeting with your mom or MIL, it is suggested that the parent who is the son or daughter take the lead. It is usually much easier for a grandparent to hear about an issue or concern if it's initially

presented by the son or daughter.

8. Tell your mom or MIL specifically what she can do to for you when she offers to help or you're requesting her help, e.g., "Please take the baby for a 45-minute walk to the park and do not let her fall asleep." (Remember to bite your tongue, or correct in a gentle, loving way if your mom or MIL gets it wrong and brings back a sleeping baby! And maybe reread #3.)

9. When your mom or MIL is babysitting, write down all the information she will need for nap time, bedtime routines, and special sleeping companions, such as stuffed animals and blankets; details for feeding schedules; rules about television programs and developmental CDs; directions for giving prescriptions and medications (have her write down the times she administers any meds); emergency numbers.

10. Make sure your mom or MIL is clear about her role when she is alone with your nanny or babysitter. If there are problems, your mom or MIL needs to know whether you want her to get involved or stay in the background.

11. Help your mom or MIL purchase appropriate car seats for her own vehicles, and show her how to install and de-install them. Same for strollers, pack 'n plays, and any other equipment you want her to use or own.

12. Suggest activities for your mom or MIL to do with your kids. You know your area and the special activities going on. Provide all the details for it to work out, e.g., print out driving directions or get GPS coordinates; give suggestions of where to park; get tickets in advance; make suggestions for restaurants the kids will like and are in line with your mom's or MIL's budget.

13. Help your mom or MIL with long-distance grandparenting.

(This is the same advice offered to grandparents.) Suggest that your mom or MIL:

- Take advantage of the Internet, especially with older grandchildren: e.g., e-mail, Skype, share photos and sites with information of places to visit together, share favorite music.
- Keep notes of what she learns from her grandchildren in phone calls or Skyping or visits, so she can reference this information in future interactions, e.g., dolls' names, their friends' names, games they like, movies they want to see. This helps the long-distance bonding and is proof positive to the grandchildren that their grandmother is listening to them and that she is interested in their lives.
- Plan things to do together the next time she'll be with the grandchildren.
- Tell her grandchildren about her hobbies, and when possible, share her hobbies, and teach them, e.g., chess, biking, knitting, baking, sailing.

14. You can never show your mom or MIL too much respect or gratitude for all she does.
15. When in doubt, lighten up!

{Readers' Comments}

Dear Readers,

I received many comments about the Do's and Don'ts for Grandmothers and the Do's and Don'ts for Young Moms.

One young mom said, *"I showed the Do's and Don'ts for Grandmothers to my mom . . . she does a great job of honoring these already. I love the ones for me [Do's and Don'ts for Young Moms], and I've shared them with my mom so she can help keep me honest."*

It sounds like the guidelines are helpful to this young mom and her mother for reviewing, affirming, and validating what they've been doing right along, working in tandem. I like the term "honoring" because this implies mutual respect and constant vigilance, the cornerstones of a strong relationship.

A grandparent presents a different perspective on the guidelines: *"Don't grandparents have a special relationship with their grandchildren that they should define, or are they only robots responding to the directions of the parents?"* The way the question is phrased sounds a bit like an either/or. That is, either the grandparents have free reign to develop their relationships with the grandchildren, or they can interact only as dictated by the parents. I agree with this grandparent that there is and should be something special that develops between a grandparent and grandchild, but the point I try to make is that this "specialness" is bounded by the tenets of the childrearing practices the parents have defined—and these practices often include rules and expectations with which the grandparent may not agree.

However, grandparents deviate at their own peril, because what they may consider "merely developing my special relationship with my grandchild" may be interpreted by the young parent as annoying, disrespectful, or critical. In short, it is not an either/or, but rather, a relationship-building process between the grandparent and grandchild that requires the grandparent to factor in, to honor, if you will, the parents' preferences and requests.

A related question: *"I am sure that the 'zip it' advice applies more to the MIL (mother-in-law) than to the mother. Do you agree?"* I can best address this question by sharing a comment from another reader, a young mom: *"I love the advice to grandmothers to 'zip it' when in doubt—always a better [course of action] than the helicopter grandparent, which really can threaten the parent's sense that he/*

she is doing the job well." Of course there may be more emotional water under the dam between a mom and her mom by virtue of the length and intensity of that relationship, but I agree with this mom's comment that it doesn't matter if a helicopter grandparent is related by biology or marriage, the impact is the same: The young parent often feels criticized. Zip it! This advice applies to both mothers and mothers-in-law.

Some additional comments and suggestions from this same young mom: *"I do think that setting clear expectations can derail the helicopter grandparent. I do, however, think that pre-planning is not always the answer. Things can (and do) come up after the baby is born—and things always change as the baby or child grows. So another thought is to periodically (post birth) check in with the daughter or daughter-in-law about expectations and guidelines."*

Excellent advice! As moms and grandmoms alike point out, the new mom with the first baby typically has a greater dependency on the guidance and advice of her mom or MIL than she does as that baby grows older and/or she has additional children. The initial, much-needed involvement of the grandmothers gets replaced over time by the young mom's firsthand experience and increased confidence in her parenting abilities.

Another young mom writes: *"I never quite knew how to describe my mother, and now I do. She is a Helicopter Grandmother, big time. We bicker a lot because she is always telling me what to do and questioning my decisions. I would love for her to read the guidelines for grandmothers, but I am sure she'll just tear them apart. Any suggestions?"*

One suggestion is that instead of positioning the guidelines as something your mother needs to read and consider, you might share them with her as something you're working on. Ask her to go over each of the Do's and Don'ts for Young Moms with you and invite her to give her opinion on how you're doing on each one. Perhaps a real dialogue can result because you would be putting the focus on yourself, not on her. A next logical step might be for your mom to at least glance at the Do's and Don'ts for Grandmothers, and if you're lucky, be open to discussing them with you.

A suggestion from a grandmother: *"The Do's and Don'ts are a very helpful and extensive list. I'm smiling as I think that both of these lists [for grandmothers and young moms] should go home with new parents everywhere when the baby leaves the hospital. Parents usually keep a feeding/pooping/peeing (fpp) record on the refrigerator—your lists will be needed infinitely longer than the fpp list."*

And a final comment from a reader, one that I think aptly summarizes what I intend as the primary purpose of the Dos and Don'ts: *"If all parents and grandparents read both sets of guidelines, it would go a long way towards helping everyone have comfortable, loving relationships—with the children the winners!"*

{Chapter 6}

My Co-Workers and I Are Having Heated Discussions about Kids' Homework

Dear Dr. Gramma Karen:

I'm a grandmother who works with several young moms. I am just amazed when I listen to them talk about "helping" their kids with their daily homework and projects. I say "helping" because what they describe is flat-out doing their kids' assignments. I think that what they should be doing instead is to help their kids set timelines and discuss resources they can use. They say their kids, even the young ones, get so much homework, most of it useless busy work, that there's not much learning from it anyway. These young parents say there is a lot of pressure and frustration around these vast amounts of homework and that is why they end up helping their kids with it.

When I've said to these parents that maybe they could talk to the teachers about the homework, they said they don't want to get on the wrong side of the teachers and get labeled a "problem parent." I worry that these kids are not learning to take responsibility for their actions or decisions. We all read your column, so I said I would write you. Can you offer some perspective and guidelines on this? That is, the parents who say their kids aren't learning from their homework anyway, so it doesn't matter if they help them vs. those who see value in homework and feel the kids should be doing their own homework, no matter what.

It is easy to see why you and your co-workers might find your discussions about homework heated and emotional. Strong opinions abound, and although there is research, as discussed below, much of it is inconclusive, so controversy is inevitable.

For example, according to Alfie Kohn, education, parenting, human behavior researcher and author, both points of view you've identified have some merit. For example, in his book *The Homework Myth: Why Our Kids Get Too Much of a Bad Thing*, his research led him to conclude that "There is absolutely no evidence of any academic benefit from assigning homework in elementary or middle school. For younger students, in fact, there isn't even a *correlation* between whether children do homework (or how much they do) and any meaningful measure of achievement. At the high school level, the correlation is weak and tends to disappear when more sophisticated statistical measures are applied. Meanwhile, no study has ever substantiated the belief that homework builds character or teaches good study habits."

The Center for Public Education, an initiative of the National School Boards Association, has also done extensive research on homework (http://www.centerforpubliceducation. org/Main-Menu/Instruction/What-research-says-about-the-value-of-homework-At-a-glance/What-research-says-about-the-value-of-homework-Research-review.html) and agrees the evidence does not support that homework results in higher academic achievement across-the-board for all groups. However, their research suggests that "Certain nonacademic benefits of homework have been shown, especially for younger students. Indeed, some primary-level teachers may assign homework for such benefits, which include learning the importance of responsibility, managing time, developing study habits, and staying with a task until it is completed."

But these supposed nonacademic benefits of homework are challenged: "There has been no research done on whether homework teaches responsibility, self-discipline, or motivation. That's just a value judgment. The counter argument can just as easily be made that homework teaches kids to cheat, do the least amount of work, or to get by." *(The End of Homework: How Homework Disrupts Families, Overburdens Children, and Limits Learning, by Etta Kralovec and John Buell.)*

However, one area of strong agreement among parents, educators, and students is that homework can be a serious family irritant. A survey done by Public Agenda, a nonprofit, nonpartisan research group (http://www.publicagenda.org/), found that 50 percent of parents surveyed said they have had a serious argument with their children over homework; 34 percent said it became a source of struggle and stress for them and their children. Others share emotional anecdotes where parent-child relationships have been seriously or permanently damaged by tensions and arguments over homework.

In light of research that questions the value of homework, especially for younger children, some educators have made important changes in homework policies. For example, one private school in Manhattan has implemented a no-homework policy before fifth grade. Many of this school's parents, even when familiar with the research on homework, are uncomfortable with this policy, fearing their children are being academically short changed. It is hard to give up the time-honored adage that more homework equals higher achievement, even when the latest research refutes this.

Perhaps most convincing is the fact that "Many of the countries with the highest scoring students on achievement tests, such as Japan, Denmark, and the Czech Republic, have teachers who assign little homework. It seems that the more homework a nation's teachers assign, the worse that nation's students do on the achievement tests (http://www.sup.org/book.cgi?id=7192).

Regarding how much homework should be assigned, The Center for Public Education and other groups currently recommend no homework in elementary school, about one hour per night in middle school, and between 1 1/2 and 2 1/2 hours a night in high school. In light of these research-based guidelines, it is understandable that many parents are angry and frustrated when their young children are forced to do an hour or more of homework each night. In fact, many parents admit they are frustrated to the point of often doing their children's homework for them.

Many educators and parents who want homework policies reevaluated in light of recent research are working together to set up task forces. Your co-workers with school-age children might talk about the feasibility of volunteering to set up and/or serve on such a task force. Many Parent Teacher Associations (PTAs) across the nation are initiating this kind of dialogue by showing the film *Race to Nowhere* (http://www.racetonowhere.com/home), described as a "film and call to mobilize families, educators, and policy makers to challenge current assumptions on how to best prepare the youth of America to become healthy, bright, contributing, and leading citizens." The follow-up discussions will no doubt include the topic of homework.

Dear Readers:

Your many responses to my article fell into two main categories. First, many were very surprised to learn that according to the latest research there is no correlation between homework and increased achievement for elementary and middle school students. This has prompted many to rethink the whole topic of homework, and hence, a second comment is that many readers want to know how to get other educators and parents to reassess their school's current homework policies.

To respond to your comments I interviewed Simone Hristidis, Head of Lower School, Columbia Grammar and Preparatory School (CGPS), located on the Upper West Side in Manhattan (http://www.cgps.org). Ms. Hristidis has been a member of the CGPS community for 26 years, first as a staff member, then serving as the director of admissions for 17 years, and for the past two years as Head of Lower School. As a recognized and respected educational leader, she was interviewed for the book *The Kindergarten Wars: The Battle to Get into America's Best Private Schools*, by Alan Eisenstock.

While at the national level the average homework load has tripled since 1981, Ms. Hristidis is responsible for implementing what she calls a "reduced and limited" homework policy for CGPS students in the lower grades. Reduced and limited homework means that the number of nights a week they have small homework assignments correlates to their grade level. For example, students in first grade get a small homework assignment one night a week, then two nights a week in second grade, et cetera, and by 4th grade they have homework Monday through Thursday. Although there is a no homework policy on weekends and vacations for all grades through middle school, pleasure reading is encouraged.

The reduced and limited homework policy focuses on reading and literature, not repetitious drills or memorization. Rather, CGPS homework assignments use reading to help teach and fortify the skills required for lifelong learning and success, including, problem solving, critical thinking, and analysis. When interviewed by Alina Adams for *Examiner.com*, Ms. Hristidis summarized her basic philosophy of education which informs her beliefs about homework: *"Learning facts without learning how (or why, or when, or if) to apply them is pointless. I'm kind of famous for always asking, no matter what the educational topic is, i.e., Traditional or progressive? Structured or nurturing? Single sex or co-ed? Private or public? That depends on what you want the end result to be."*

Ms. Hristidis's advocacy for reduced and limited homework started when her oldest child, who just graduated college, was in 4th grade. She stepped back and looked at her child's typical day: in school all day until mid afternoon, followed by sports and other lessons until 6 p.m. Then her exhausted child was looking at a couple hours of homework—assignments that were just busy work, increasing pressure and frustration, but not helping with academic achievement. She concluded, "We're killing our kids with homework." Although she would rather see a total no-homework policy through the 4th grade, she realized that if she was to bring about any changes, she would need to compromise with a reduced and limited homework policy.

When I asked Ms. Hristidis if she encountered resistance from the CGPS staff and/or parents to reduce the amount of homework assigned, especially in light of the typical homework trend that "more is better," she explained that as the director of admissions for so many years she was in an ideal position to help parents interested in CGPS to understand the school's reduced and limited homework policies during the application process. Parents seeking a program with heavy doses of homework at the younger ages were helped to appreciate that CGPS would not be a good fit for their children.

Occasionally, Ms. Hristidis encounters parents who tend to blame the reduced and limited homework policy for various undesirable outcomes, e.g., the parent who believed that his child did not get into an honors class because he didn't have enough homework in the lower grades, the parent who says that her child is watching too much TV or spending too much time on the computer because there "isn't enough homework."

Also, parents will at times need reassurance that their children will quickly adopt good study habits in their middle and high school years if they haven't had rigorous homework demands in their earlier years. To this particular concern the latest brain research indicates that there is no decrease in academic achievement or a lack of adaption of good study habits when homework is deferred to later school years (*The Homework Myth: Why Our Kids Get Too Much of a Bad Thing*, Alfie Kohn). Fortunately, these instances of parental resistance are rare and have not decreased from the overall acceptance of the reduced and limited homework policy.

For those educators and parents who want to initiate a conversation about the homework policies in their educational communities, Ms. Hristidis encourages them to rent the movie *Race to Nowhere* (http://www.racetonowhere.com/home). She says that although it isn't a perfect movie, it does pack a powerful message about the detrimental aspects of homework.

All the Lower School teachers at CGPS viewed the film; all the parents were invited to see it, many of whom did. She said viewing and discussing this movie were very helpful in laying the foundation for implementing the reduced and limited homework policy now in place at Columbia Grammar and Preparatory School. It helped everyone get more comfortable with the idea of "less is better" when it comes to the important topic of homework in the lower and middle school years.

{Chapter 7}

My Grandson Is No Longer Loving Towards Me

Dear Dr. Gramma Karen:

This letter concerns my relationship with my eight-year-old grandson Matt. For the first five years of his life I cared for Matt several times a week, until he reached school age. We had a wonderful and loving relationship. At age five his parents divorced—a mean and difficult divorce. Matt's mother played him against my husband and me until my son's lawyer, a child advocate, wrote up legal papers that said neither party could talk badly to Matt about family members. Matt seems to have adjusted very well to the divorce, and I must say both his parents are loving people and are doing a good job of parenting.

However, something has drastically changed in his attitude towards me, and on occasion, towards my husband, his granddad. I used to be one of my grandson's favorite people—we were very close— but starting around the time of his parents' divorce three years ago, he became rude and shunned me in front of others. As soon as I approach him for a hello or a hug, he cringes; he is not this way with others. His parents have occasionally chastised him if they see him acting disrespectfully.

I don't know if I should have a talk with my grandson or my son, or if I should just ignore it and hope that in time we become close again. Meanwhile, I don't want to make things worse. I think it is unusual that a grandchild seemingly abhors a grandparent with whom he was so close.

It is difficult to know how a five-year-old processes what's going on around him when his parents are going through a divorce. However, here is what is known: Approximately 80 percent of children of divorced parents become well-adjusted, successful adults with the memories of that painful time playing less a role in their lives as they get older. The other 20 percent of these children experience a variety of psychological and social difficulties that can affect their well being in significant ways, sometimes into their adult lives.

Although you describe Matt as currently doing well three years after the divorce, it is possible Matt falls into this latter group. The fact that a child advocate was required to rein in the emotional cauldron of contentiousness and nastiness swirling around him suggests he experienced a lot of stuff he wasn't able to understand. It is typical for young children in this situation to respond in a variety of ways, including, drawing erroneous conclusions such as "I must have been a bad boy and caused the divorce," fantasizing his parents will reunite, or worrying about not being taken care of or being abandoned.

Many grandparents play a pivotal role in their grandchild's life. For example, one study indicated that the grandparent-grandchild relationship is, in fact, second in emotional importance only to the parent-child relationship. As a primary caretaker for

Matt for his first five years, it is possible that you were and remain a safety net for him. So, although things seem to have outwardly stabilized for Matt with his parents, this does not mean things have internally and emotionally stabilized for him. Perhaps he heard something said about you that has left him upset with or confused about you and/or he is redirecting his anger, confusion, and fears related to his parents' divorce to you. Perhaps his shunning you and withholding his affection may be a safe outlet for him to release negative emotions because you are an emotional rock for him and he intuitively knows you will absorb his acting out.

Will he drift back to you over time? It's a good possibility, but I'm going to suggest you be more proactive, especially since it sounds like your son would support you. My suggestion is that you locate and work with a professional who specializes in children of divorce, e.g., therapist, psychologist, psychiatrist. If you don't have your own resources for locating one, you can Google "child divorce psychologists in [your city and state]," or "child or family therapists who specialize in divorce in [your city and state]." I urge you to talk with several of them and then decide which one you'd like to work with.

I think it will be advantageous if you position your working with a professional as something you and your husband are doing for yourselves, your son, and grandson, and not make Matt the focal point. Rather, you can talk about getting therapy because you are grandparents in a family that has experienced significant and difficult change, and you want to make sure you are doing all you can to be supportive, loving, and good parents for your son and as grandparents for your grandson.

Over time your therapist will establish his/her own relationship with each of you. He/she is trained to help Matt articulate how he is feeling about his parents' divorce and help him sort out and work through anything troubling him or falling into the category of "unfinished business," including his relationship with you and your husband.

Matt most certainly abhors the divorce and the breakup of his parents, but I doubt he abhors you. I agree with you that something has changed in his behavior towards you, and it is likely that he is afraid to express certain feelings and/or doesn't know what is bothering him or how to talk safely about it. A good therapist can help you, your husband, your son, and your grandson—as individuals and as a family unit—better understand how the difficult divorce affected each of you and may still be affecting you, and what you might do going forward.

PART 2

Communication
The Need To Get It Right

{Chapter 8}

I Have to Tell My Children Their Grandmother Has Cancer

Dear Dr. Gramma Karen:

My mother-in-law, with whom my seven-year-old daughter and eight-year-old son are close, has just been diagnosed with lymphoma cancer. What advice do you have for what we tell them about their grandmother's health situation?

I want you to know how very sorry I am about your mother-in-law's diagnosis.

As a young parent, statistics indicate that you are not alone in having to tell your children about a member of your family facing a serious medical issue, especially regarding grandparents. For example, the National Center for Health Statistics recently released annual data on numbers and causes of deaths of people over 65 (comprising the major grandparent population). Of 1.8 million deaths in this 65 + age group: 25 percent of the deaths (450,000) were caused by heart disease; 23 percent (414,000) caused by cancer; 7 percent (126,000) by strokes; and the remaining deaths due to smaller percentages of other diseases and illnesses. This means that many young parents will be asking the question you have posed: How do I tell my child that a grandparent or other close family member has a serious disease or illness? In response to your question I've developed a set of 14 guidelines for you and other young parents.

Guidelines for Telling Your Child that a Family Member Has a Serious Disease or Illness

1. Prepare in advance what you want to say to your child. If you have more than one child, you may want to talk with each child individually first, especially if there are wide age differences, and then talk as a family. Talking with each child individually has the advantage of making it easier for you to customize your message for him/her, as well as make it easier for your child to ask questions without sibling distractions. It is important to meet as a family to review the message, share information and concerns, and provide opportunities to ask questions.

2. Your goal is to tell your child the truth in a way he/she can understand.

3. Your child will be paying special attention to your nonverbal communication, so you want to be as calming as possible. Share your feelings, but also emphasize how diseases and illnesses are a natural part of life. You may want to talk about the range of emotions you feel to make it easier for your child to express his/her emotions, e.g., sad, angry, confused, guilty, anxious, curious, positive, hopeful.

4. Before you talk with your child, you may want to find out from the person with the disease or illness if he/she has some preferences about what gets communicated about his/her situation and his/her thoughts about having visitors and/or

involvement with your child.

5. Here is a suggested format to follow in your communication with your child:

- Opening: "We have some family news we want to share with you. We'll explain what's going on and then answer any questions you might have."
- The situation or diagnosis: "Grandma has learned from her doctors that . . . "
- Explanation of the diagnosis:
  i. Use medically correct terminology, e.g., cancer, congestive heart failure, and then explain the disease or illness in language they can understand.
  ii. Show them by pointing to your own body where the disease is located and/or use illustrations from books or pamphlets or hand-drawn pictures.
- Explanation of the treatment, its duration, and possible side effects.
- Prognosis or what the medical team is saying the likely or possible outcomes will be.

6. If your child asks you something and you're not sure or don't know the answer, write it down on a piece of paper in front of him/her and say you'll find out. Explain how you'll get the answer and then follow through as soon as possible.

7. Encourage your child to ask questions and share emotions; you will want to empathize as he/she expresses a full range of possible feelings, concerns, and anxieties.

8. Your child's main questions and concerns may have to do with death: "Will Grandma die?" "Will you die?" "Will I die?" When talking with a child about whether someone will die from cancer (or any life-threatening medical condition) The American Cancer Society has examples of what might

be said (in these examples I use "Grandma" as the person diagnosed):

- "Sometimes people do die from cancer. We're not expecting that to happen because the doctors have told us they have very good treatments these days, and Grandma's type of cancer usually does go away with treatment."
- "The doctors have told us that Grandma's chances of being cured are very good. We're going to believe that until we have reason to believe something else. We hope you can believe that too. We'll tell you if we find out anything new or different."
- "There is no way to know right now what's going to happen. We'll know more after the first treatments are finished. When we know more, we'll be sure to tell you."
- "Right now there's not a lot known about the kind of cancer Grandma has. But Grandma is going to give it her best shot and do everything she can to get well."
- "Grandma's cancer is a hard one to treat but she's going to do everything she can to get better. No one can know right now what will happen down the road. What you can be sure of is that we'll be honest with you about what is going on. If you can't stop worrying, please tell me so that we can work on that together."

9. Help your child figure out ways he/she can show his/her love and support, e.g., draw a picture, make a thinking-of-you card, talk on the phone, Skype, play cards or a game when visiting, watch TV together, change the water in the vase with flowers.

10. Based on your child's needs and personality, let him/her know when you will update him/her on how the family member is doing, e.g., whenever you learn anything, every

Friday after doctors' appointments. One child may need to get updates whenever they're available. Another child may handle things better with a set day and time to talk about the situation and what's changed.

11. Let your child know whether it is okay for him/her to talk about this news and with whom, e.g., cousins, friends, teachers. Help him/her figure out what to say when talking about it with others.

12. This is most important: Most children like routine and structure, so you'll want to be ready to talk about changes affecting the child and the family that may/will happen as a result of the loved one's illness or disease. Examples:

• "Because Grandma will be tired from her treatments and will need lots of rest, she won't be able to take you to your swim lessons like she's been doing."

• "Grandma will be having her treatments during the summer, so she won't be going with us to the cabin for vacation."

• "I will be taking Grandma to her doctors' appointments three days a week, so I will not be with you on those afternoons, but Aunt Susan will be with you."

13. Equally important, talk with your child about changes he/she may see as a result of your loved one's treatments and/or operations. These changes may include visible side effects, new people in the picture, e.g., caretakers, people servicing devices and equipment.

• "Grandma will be taking some very strong medicines to help fight the disease. One side effect of the medicine is that she may lose some or all of her hair, eyebrows, and eyelashes. Sometimes she may wear a wig or scarf on her head, and other times you may see her 'looking bald.' Her hair should grow back later."

- "When we visit Grandma at her home, she may have a nurse or nurse's aide staying with her to help take care of her."
- "Grandma will have to take some of her medicine intravenously. Here is a picture of what this will look like and this is what it means . . ."

14. Your child will probably need lots of reassurances that:
- He/she did not in any way cause the family member's medical condition.
- The family member's medical condition is not contagious and they don't have to worry that they or anyone else in the family will catch it.
- Yes, there may be changes as a result of the diagnosis, but everyone will continue to love each other and help each other as much as possible.

In closing, I want to emphasize that as difficult as this communication about Grandma's health situation is, and will continue to be in the future, the key is to give your children truthful information when they need it to help them cope as well as possible from day to day.

{Readers Share Their Experiences}

Dear Readers:

After dealing with the situation of telling her two children that their grandmother had cancer, Laurie, the young mother who was looking for advice, e-mailed me an update regarding my second guideline, "Your goal is to tell your child the truth in a way he/she can understand." She wrote that she found her seven-year-old daughter can get easily overwhelmed so Laurie is careful not to share too much of the medical details with her, whereas her eight-year-old can handle the medical details. Further, she suggests that children not conduct their own, unsupervised online searches for information because sites contain graphic images that can be extremely upsetting.

Another reader, a grandmother who underwent a long and painful cancer treatment regimen wrote about losing her hair: *"The grandchildren got pretty used to seeing me with and without my wig, but sometimes they weren't so sure about me without it. One of my grandsons saw me without my wig when he went in for a nap, and then with it on when he woke up. He exclaimed, 'Grandma's hair grew back!'"* This is a reminder that sometimes we need to be more specific in explaining time frameworks to children!

Regarding guideline #13, about talking with your child about changes he/she may see as a result of your loved one's treatments and/or operations, this same grandmother wrote: *"At one point I carried around my chemo in a tote bag all day, every day, for about a week, because my grandchildren had some end-of-school activities that I didn't want to miss. I think my grandchildren just accepted this because I was pretty nonchalant about it."*

In response to the last guideline, "Yes, there may be changes as a result of the diagnosis, but everyone will continue to love each other and help each other as much as possible," she wrote, *"I think this is key. My daughter made a poster-size photo of my grandchildren to hang by my station in the clinic for the two weeks I was there for a difficult procedure. This poster not only cheered me immeasurably, but all the other patients and staff loved it."*

Another reader wrote: *"I wish I had read your fourth guideline a couple of years ago* ("Before you talk with your child, you may want to find out from the person with the disease or illness if he/

she has some preferences about what gets communicated about his/her situation and his/her thoughts about having visitors and/or involvement with your child"), *as I brought my kids into the hospital as a surprise to see my father after he had some surgery. He was very angry with me, saying he did not want his grandchildren to see him that way. I should have checked with him first."*

A final positive comment from a young mom whose mother underwent cancer treatments and is currently enjoying good health: *"The children can actually come away from an experience like this [when a sick person struggles and survives] relieved and with a positive feeling that people get sick or have life struggles—but that help is available."* I would add that even when the outcome results in losing a loved one, children can still find a sense of comfort and encouragement in seeing how their family members and friends all pull together to offer love and support.

{Chapter 9}

I Worry My Son's Inheritance Is at Risk

Dear Dr. Gramma Karen:

When I was in my teens, I was wild and out of control. I got pregnant and decided to raise my son Robert on my own. (His biological father is not and will not ever be a part of his life.) When Robert was a few months old, I meet Steve, a truly wonderful, decent, and reliable man. I told Steve everything about my past. We got married when Robert was around two, and one of the first things Steve did after we were married was to legally adopt Robert, who is now six. We have another son, Allan, who is four.

I am a happy stay-at-home mom. Steve is a school teacher, so although we manage financially, we don't have a lot of money. But Steve's parents do, and here is the problem. Although Steve's parents are always nice to Robert and generous with gifts, they obviously feel he is not Steve's "real" son because in their wills, we just found out, they have left significant amounts of money to Allan and their two other grandchildren, Steve's sister's children, but they have left nothing to Robert.

As a result, Steve does not want them to leave anything to Allan because he says, "I have two sons. Either they both inherit, or neither of them does." I think this is crazy because money is money and it will help one of our sons. Steve is being stubborn and we're really at odds over this.

When you described your husband as "truly wonderful, decent, and reliable," you forgot to add that he is also highly principled, at least in this particular situation, meaning his personal rules for guiding his behavior and conduct seem firm. Ethicists, who specialize in ethics and moral behavior, define these behavioral standards as "governing principles." It appears Steve's governing principle is that he wants equal treatment for both his sons. It seems your governing principle is to do whatever you can to help your offspring be more secure financially, in this case by accepting a gift that is being offered to one of your two sons.

The ethicist would say you and Steve have competing governing principles, meaning both of them cannot be enacted simultaneously: Both your sons cannot be treated equally if one of your sons inherits and the other does not. As long as you both hold on to your governing principles as currently professed, they will continue to compete and you have a stalemate. So the challenge is how you might address this impasse.

One option is to do nothing, that is, just let events play out according to the terms set out in Steve's parents' will, and deal with the situation when you have to, and that could be decades into the future. The advantage to this strategy is that both your governing principles are dormant—no discussion, no clashes. Also, in the meantime, advantageous changes could happen, e.g., Steve's parents rewrite their wills to include both your sons, or one or both of you modify your position. The downside of deferring and taking a wait-and-see stance is that things being left unresolved could cause one or both of you frustration and/or resentment, either of which could stress your relationship over this issue even more.

Another option, one that troubles me to have to even mention, is that one of you gives the other an ultimatum: "Accept my position or else . . ." We don't have to dwell on how unpleasant and unproductive this could become, but it is an option.

A third option is that you and Steve work together to try and come up with what our ethicist calls a "bridging principle," that is, a behavioral action that connects both your governing principles and still reflects your core values and morals. For example, depending on Steve's relationship with his parents and his comfort level in discussing their wills with them, he might ask if they would consider taking the amount they planned to leave to Allan and split it between Robert and Allan.

It would be a delicate discussion, but if Steve can successfully express appreciation for their generosity and explain that it is important to him that both his sons are treated equally vis-à-vis their wills, they might understand Steve's request and agree to it. Another potential benefit of having a discussion with them is that it is possible they excluded Robert based on an erroneous assumption, for example, assuming that Robert's biological father would be playing some role in Robert's finances. However, when all is said and done, we are talking about Steve's parents' money and they can do with it whatever pleases them.

Another possible bridging principle is for your husband to match from his own inheritance, assuming he receives something from his parents, the amount Allan inherits and give it to Robert. This strategy does not change the fact that Steve's parents singled out one grandson with a favoring circumstance, but it does result in both boys being treated equally in terms of the dollar amounts they receive.

Whatever you and Steve decide to do, you might ask yourselves some questions about your decision. For example:

- Would you feel comfortable explaining your decision to your children when they're old enough to understand?
- Would you want your children to make the same decision if they were faced with your situation?
- Does your decision honor your core values and morals?
- Does your decision leave you free of resentment and/or anger towards your spouse?

If you can both answer yes to those four questions, you will probably feel at peace with the agreed-upon decision.

{ Steve Provides an Update }

Dear Readers:

Steve decided to talk with his parents about how he felt about one of his sons being excluded in their wills, and both Steve and his wife are very glad he did! Steve learned that his parents had drafted their own wills and had not as yet shared them with their lawyer. It seems Steve's parents remembered seeing some TV show in which the biological parent of an adopted child had caused all kinds of inheritance problems when the adoptive parents died, and they were afraid something similar could happen in their family. Steve's sister had seen their draft (because her husband was being named executor) and before discussing it with her parents who were traveling, she told Steve about Robert not inheriting with the other grandchildren. Steve says his sister is a good person and he does not think she was trying to start any trouble; she was merely sharing what she had read.

Steve's parents were unsure what to do about Robert's

inheritance. The TV show they had seen rattled them and they planned to discuss it with their lawyer. They were glad Steve talked with them. They reassured him that they love Robert and consider him their grandchild right along their other grandchildren. Their wills are in the hands of their lawyer, who reassured them that Robert's biological father cannot legally cause any mischief. Therefore, Steve's parents' last wills and testaments will be executed with all four grandchildren inheriting equally. Love happy endings! P.S. Things are not always what they seem to be.

{Chapter 10}

My Friend Has Cut Herself Off from Her Grandchildren

Dear Dr. Gramma Karen:

My friends Sally and Mark never saw their grandchildren (ages five and seven) until a year ago. The family estrangement happened nine years ago when Sally and Mark's son Ronnie was getting married to Emily.

Ronnie and Emily had planned their wedding to take place on a cruise ship with family and some close friends in attendance. Then, three weeks before the wedding, Sally's mother (Ronnie's grandmother), who suffered from congestive heart failure for many years, took a turn for the worse. The hospital staff said she most likely was not going to survive. Sally told Ronnie and Emily that she and Mark would not be leaving her mother's side.

Ronnie asked his parents what he should do about the wedding plans and Sally said, "You need to do what you need to do." Ronnie and Emily decided to go ahead with their wedding on the cruise ship. While they were away, Sally's mother died. Sally was so upset that Ronnie was off getting married while his grandmother was dying that she vowed she would never speak to him again, and she didn't until a year ago when Mark finally convinced her to reconnect with Ronnie, Emily, and their two grandchildren.

Things are still a bit strained, and they now get together occasionally, but Sally is having a hard time forgiving Ronnie. People who know about the situation tend to agree with Sally that Ronnie should have changed his wedding plans. I'm curious what you think.

I can see why many would agree with Sally at first blush that Ronnie should have postponed his wedding because of his grandmother's medical crisis, but I find myself wanting to be an advocate for Ronnie. He most likely, and correctly, anticipated one of three responses when he asked his mother for her advice about what to do about his wedding. The most obvious response would be that his mother would tell him that she would like him to postpone the wedding. In fact, many parents would probably agree with her that it would be disrespectful for him to be getting married while his grandmother was dying.

However, another possible response could be that because she, Sally, would be staying bedside with her mother, and although this meant she would miss the cruise and wedding, she nevertheless wanted Ronnie and Emily to go ahead with their plans to get married. Granted, many would be uncomfortable with this option, but some parents would encourage going forward with the nuptials because it is their philosophical conviction that because life comprises both sad and joyous events and because we cannot always control their timing, there are times it makes sense to experience them simultaneously. In fact, for many, the experience of joyous nuptials could make dealing with the loss of a loved one easier.

The third possible response actually took place when Ronnie asked his mother what he should do, and she answered, "You need to do what you need to do," implying that whatever he decided to do would be acceptable to her. "You decide" is all well and good.

However, as Ronnie discovered, that was not the case. Sally, in fact, mislead Ronnie. She wanted Ronnie to put his wedding on hold, but this is not what she communicated to him, so there was no discussion, no sharing of emotions or attempts at understanding each other's position on the matter. This, sadly, is what happens when people are not honest and forthright in expressing themselves and expect others to figure out what they really mean, in effect, read their minds. Taken to an extreme, it can become a form of "If you truly loved me, you would know what I really mean."

Granted, Sally was responding to Ronnie's question during an exceptionally emotional and difficult time, and perhaps the thought of Ronnie and Emily celebrating their wedding as her mother was dying may have struck her as totally imponderable. Her feelings are understandable, but her true feelings are not what she communicated. You asked me what I think. I think Sally, and Sally alone, created the estrangement that caused her and the family so much unnecessary pain.

Further, you say she is having a hard time forgiving her son, and this suggests to me that she still sees herself as being on the receiving end of an injustice, rather than viewing herself as the initiator of the problem. The more appropriate question is: Has her son forgiven her for her dishonesty in answering his question about what she would have preferred he do all those many years ago? At least the three generations are now spending time together, and that's a start. Here's hoping more honest communications are part of their interactions.

In closing, I want to share another family's story involving an incapacitated grandmother and her granddaughter's wedding. This particular grandmother fell as she was getting dressed on the morning of her granddaughter's wedding, breaking her hip and ending up in the emergency room, tended to by her son-in-law. The grandmother insisted that her situation not ruin her granddaughter's wedding, so with the son-in-law and two other family members sworn to secrecy, the wedding took place. People were told the grandmother had an adverse reaction to her routine pills and would get to the wedding as soon as possible.

After the wedding and reception, everyone was told the truth about the grandmother's absence. The bride, groom, and wedding party decided that if the grandmother couldn't come to the party, they would take the party to her. To the delight of the grandmother, as well as the staff and other patients, they arrived at the hospital in their full wedding garb. Indeed, this wedding party did what it needed to do!

{Chapter 11}

My Granddaughter's Secret Is Distressing Me

Dear Dr. Gramma Karen:

A few months ago my granddaughter Ruth, with whom I am very close, asked me if I would promise not to tell anyone if she told me something. I agreed. She told me that she is dating Kip, a young man she met at college. The problem is that he is not of our religion or ethnic background. Ruth said her mom (my daughter Sandra) and dad would disown her if they knew. I am sorry to say that I think Ruth may be right.

My late husband and I were more secular than religious and that is how we raised Sandra. However, Sandra met and married a very religious man from a very religious family, and although they tried to raise Ruth to be observant and she has always been respectful of her parents' ways, she never seemed committed the way they are.

I am heartsick over this situation. I fear Sandra will never forgive me for knowing about Ruth and Kip dating and not telling her. Kip's family is accepting of the situation and they make Ruth feel welcome in their home. Kip and Ruth are now talking about getting married. I just don't know what to do.

The potentially dangerous, yet irresistible, If – Then: "If you promise not to tell anyone, then I will tell you something." Or, "If I tell you something, then you have to promise not to tell anyone." Either way, saying yes, without posing some conditions or asking some questions before committing, can result in being an unwitting party to something clandestine, secretive, and often, destructive. Alas, so many of us have been there!

If you had the luxury of responding anew to Ruth's request to share something with you in confidence, based on your current situation, would you handle things differently? For example, some might respond to Ruth's request to keep a secret by saying, "You need to know that I don't keep secrets from my spouse." Others would perhaps want to know what was expected of them: "Why do you want to tell me something confidential? What am I supposed to do with this secret information?" Some might say they are not comfortable making a commitment when they don't know what they're committing to, while others might point out that they do not want to find themselves burdened with information that could compromise them or others in any way.

Of course, all of this may be retrospectively instructive and helpful in future situations in which you are invited to become part of a secret, but now that you have made a commitment to your granddaughter not to tell, what can you do?

Before we discuss your options, I want to suggest that you and Ruth need to have a conversation about why she shared her secret with you in the first place, assuming her reasons are clear to her. It may be a simple matter of her knowing you would not reject her, that is, her wanting an ally as she travels a road that could end in estrangement from her family. Or it could be she is hoping you can play some role in getting her parents to be accepting of Kip. Yes, I strongly urge you and Ruth to have a heart-to-heart talk. If

Ruth is old enough to think about marriage, she is certainly old enough to be responsible and accountable for her decisions and to understand the position you are in.

With regard to your options, I see three. First, a more passive strategy is that you simply honor your promise to Ruth, but understand and be ready to accept that you, along with your granddaughter and her intended, may be rejected by your daughter and/or son-in-law. If you go this route, you do stand to retain the love and affection of Ruth. Another possibility is that Ruth and Kip break up and Ruth's parents never learn about it, and in the future, you make sure you don't become involved in secrets in ways that are not acceptable to you.

Second, as Ruth and Kip move in the direction of an engagement and marriage, you could be a resource by helping them show confidence in the choices they are making by transitioning from their current deception to acknowledging their relationship to Ruth's parents. In this case, with Ruth's permission, you can try to use the knowledge she entrusted to you to build bridges of understanding between Ruth, Kip, and both sets of their parents. It will be obvious to Sandra that Ruth confided in you, but it should also be clear to her that you were trying to facilitate some change and acceptance.

You may have to remind Sandra that you and her father did not threaten her with rejection when she chose to be more observant than you are. There can be a tendency to assume that more observance is preferable to being less so, but when the outcome is rejection and withholding of love, this can be a debatable assumption. In this scenario, you stand to retain Ruth's love and affection as she will understand you were trying to help, but you may lose Sandra's if she focuses on the fact that you had this knowledge for a while.

Third, you could decide to break your promise to Ruth and share your knowledge with Sandra about Ruth and Kip's relationship. Sandra may or may not forgive you for not telling her sooner, so although your relationship with Sandra may be intact, chances are Ruth will feel you have betrayed her, even if you tell her in advance that you're going to tell her mother about her dating Kip. You could permanently lose Ruth's trust.

I close with a final comment: Your choices and decisions will be driven by your personal values, your hoped-for outcomes, and the risks you are willing or unwilling to take. When secrets are involved, people's responses, even those whom we think we know well and whose behavior we think we can predict, sometimes disappoint us, sometimes surprise us, often please us, and if we're really lucky, delight us. I hope you are pleased, if not delighted, with how things turn out for you and your family.

{ Readers' Comments }

Dear Readers:

I received many comments. One reader began her response with, *"Well—this is really a hot topic!"* I think what makes it hot is that it has several threads to it: the whole idea of secrets; the topic of religion as the source of the secret; the possibility of a secretive daughter being disowned by her parents.

With regard to the general topic of secrets, several readers said they like and will use the idea of not immediately getting pulled into someone's secrets by asking some questions up front and setting some boundaries, this being especially relevant to one reader because *"Impulsive people like me always agree without knowing to what we are agreeing."* Another reader points out, *"I can appreciate the temptation of wanting to be a granddaughter's confidante—and wanting to help if help is needed—and not thinking of possible consequences beforehand."* A young mother wrote: *"I think the best advice is to always tell the child that you aren't sure you can keep the secret until you know what it is . . . and that you will always keep him or her safe, and to let them know beforehand that you will tell the secret if it has to do with safety!"*

All respondents agreed that the time had come for the grandmother to stop being part of the daughter's secret, with one reader taking this strong position: *"The grandparent can do all in her power to end the relationship between Ruth and Kip by siding with the parents and explaining the pain that the relationship will cause to all."* Another reader suggested the grandmother take the burden off herself and put it on the granddaughter: *"I hope in their heart-to-heart conversation that the grandmother explains how uncomfortable she is now that she has had time to think about things and that she hopes Ruth will go and tell her folks."* Another reader would impose a time limit and an ultimatum: *"[If I were the grandmother]. . . I would tell the grandchild she has a week to talk with her parents or I will have to disclose the relationship."*

With regard to parents disowning a child if they marry outside their ethnic or religious group, one reader, we'll call her Harriet, shared her story about being the disowned child in this kind of situation. Harriet's parents told her that they would never speak to her again if she married outside of their religion, and true to their word, Harriet's parents did disown her when she married the man anyway. Harriet and her husband have a good marriage and together they raised three children who grew up never having met their maternal grandparents. The children were always told the truth about why they had one set of grandparents in their lives and not two sets.

A couple of years ago Harriet's parents shared with one of their religious leaders the story of their disowning their daughter. The religious leader told them that disowning Harriet was wrong and that they should reach out to her and her family to make amends. Harriet talked with her husband and their three young adult children about the invitation from the grandparents to reconnect, leaving the decision up to the kids, all of whom decided to decline. *"My kids did not feel animosity or bitterness towards my parents, their grandparents—they felt nothing towards them. They just weren't motivated to welcome them into their lives."* Harriet's story is sad for so many reasons, and is a reminder that "my way, or the highway," especially when it involves something as personal and subjective as a choice of religion, can unnecessarily and permanently tear families apart.

On a brighter note, another reader shared her story about her husband's grandmother, Mama. *"Back in the early 1960s, the daughter of one of Mama's dear friends became engaged to a Jewish fellow, an act back then received as akin to sacrilege in their Irish Catholic family and community. Mama declared, 'As long as he is good to Maureen, I don't care what religion he is.' Mama was the family matriarch and so everyone who knew her adopted that philosophy. Maureen and her husband's marriage remained solid until his death."* Mama got it right!

{Chapter 12}

My Husband Refuses to Get His Legal Affairs in Order

Dear Readers,

Young parents and grandparents alike have communicated to me various issues related to wills, living wills, long-term healthcare, and arrangements for death.

For example, one grandmother says, *"For the life of me I cannot get my husband to talk about his wishes regarding his death and remains. Even though we're only in our early 70s, I think we need to talk about it."* A young parent writes about her mother-in-law's serious stroke, *"The good thing is that she has a medical surrogate and a living will. Luckily we have a doctor in the family and all the paperwork in hand since emotions are running high and different siblings feel differently. It truly is a blessing to not put the burden on the children of what to do."*

The key word to both situations is burden, meaning a load, a weight, an encumbrance. When grandparents do not deal with making their wishes known regarding medical care they want, do not want, or their end-of-life and post-death preferences, they create unnecessary burdens on their children and grandchildren. We can waste time talking about all the reasons these important issues do not get addressed—they are uncomfortable, they are reminders of one's mortality, they're anxiety provoking—but to avoid them is simply, and please forgive me for scolding, irresponsible.

We've all heard of situations in which family members are gathered around a beloved family member arguing about whether to begin or continue use of life-prolonging technology or to have a questionable operation done. Then there are the family squabbles about cremation versus traditional burial or to have a religious service or a nonreligious event. All of this stress and strain on family members is avoidable.

To the grandmother above who wants to address these issues but her husband is unwilling, I say: Be responsible and make your own arrangements, without the involvement of your husband. Your husband can do his own explaining to family members why he thinks it is okay to dump all these important decisions on them. (Sadly, he's not alone in procrastinating or avoiding, as 57 percent of adults in the United States do not have a will!)

For those grandparents who want to get their affairs in order, working with a lawyer is an obvious option, but for those who prefer to take care of their legal documents themselves before getting a lawyer involved, there are several commercial sites that can help store and sort relevant documents and accounts, including organizemyaffairs.com, estatedocsorganizer.com, legacylocker. com, aftersteps.com and safeboxfinancial.com (fees ranging from $14.95 to $59.95 to purchase the documents).

Another Web site worth checking out was started by Chanel Reynolds, a young mom who lost her husband to a tragic accident and found herself totally unprepared to deal with any of the legal aftermath. Her site can be found under http://getyourxxxxtogether. org with a not-so-nice, but very descriptive word where you see the four x's. It provides free templates for wills, living wills, powers of attorney, death, and burial planning. The site is well organized and easy to use, and to repeat, it is free.

In addition to getting one's affairs in order, it is important to communicate with family members what legal arrangements have been addressed and how to act on them. Regarding their deaths, here is an e-mail that one set of grandparents, Sharon and Barry, sent:

Dear family and special friends,

We know, we know . . . talking about what you need to do if you happen to be with us when we die isn't the most fun topic, but if you happen to be with either of us when we die (and we hope it's not for a long time), all you have to do is call Marty at:

Marty's Funeral Home

(Complete address with phone, fax, e-mail and Web site information)

Marty Smith will know exactly what to do, as we finalized all the arrangements with him today. Doesn't matter where we are in the world—just CALL MARTY, night or day, and he will take over, starting with our organ donations and harvesting, preparation of our remains, shipping, et cetera.

All decisions are made and everything is paid for. The only decision our children will have to deal with is when to have a party. We both want a party with lots of laughter, music, dancing, and good food.

You can skip the next few paragraphs if knowing what arrangements we've made is more detail than you want or need . . .

After thinking about it for about three minutes, Sharon

decided she will be cremated and her ashes will be spread in the garden at Memorial Park. She has elected not to have any family or friends deal with her ashes in any way.

After much thought, deliberation, and research, Barry is having a "green burial," which means he will not be cremated, nor will his remains receive any chemicals. Rather, he will be placed in a box of natural material and buried in a special cemetery with unmarked plots where he will become one with nature.

Barry's way is Very Barry. Sharon's way is, well, cheaper.

Just remember: when our time us up, Call Marty!

Love,

Sharon and Barry

As difficult as it was for some of the recipients to read this e-mail, it was important to Sharon and Barry that they take care of these important matters and give their children the peace of mind they deserved. After reading what became known as the Just-Call-Marty e-mail, Sharon's dear friend Lonnie wrote her: "Many cultures honor death in beautiful ways. Your preparedness for that part of life's journey is commendable. You did a fabulous job of explaining it to us, with laughter a part of it. I promise you that I will help the children plan the party."

A young mom wrote after the death of her mother-in-law: "Having people feel left out, or being forced to make decisions that the whole family is not completely on board for can destroy the remaining

family forever once a loved one is gone, and that is a true tragedy!"
Indeed. Grandparents, make sure your affairs are in order. Doing so will be greatly appreciated by your children and grandchildren.

{Chapter 13}

My Sister-in-Law Feels Guilty about a School Decision She Made

Dear Dr. Gramma Karen:

My sister-in-law Barbara is the mother of two girls, Beth, 10, and Catherine, 6. Beth attended Private School A from nursery school through grade 3, at which time she was accepted into Private School B last year; she loves her new school. (Private School A goes only through grade 6, so she would have had to made a change anyway in a couple of years, but she made friends at dance class with some girls at Private School B and decided to apply early.) Catherine stayed at Private School A last year and had a very good year.

The problem for Barbara is that having her girls in two different schools last year in different parts of the city was a scheduling and transportation nightmare, between getting the girls to their schools in the morning and to their afternoon activities and doing the pickups.

Barbara and her husband agreed life would be easier for the family if the girls were in the same school. Catherine applied to Private School B and was accepted. Now Catherine is saying she doesn't want to go to the new school and wants to stay in Private School A. Barbara is feeling guilty about removing Catherine from a school she really likes and is thinking about telling Catherine to try the new school and if she's not happy there, she can go back to her old school. (Private School A said they would be happy to have her back.) Barbara's husband thinks it would be unwise to tell Catherine she can go back to her old school if she wants to. Your thoughts?

Barbara's situation is a good reminder of the importance of parents establishing when their children are young how decision making works in their family. There are three main modes of decision making in a family: (1) the child makes the decision; (2) the parent makes the decision; (3) the parent is open to the child's influence, but ultimately makes the decision.

With regard to the first mode of decision making in a family, there are times it is not only appropriate, but desirable, for the child to make the decision. After all, helping children to learn how to make good decisions is a major parental responsibility. When the decision is to be made by the child, the parent says, "This is your decision to make." Of course the parent is available to offer more detail and provide guidance, but the intent is for the child to make the decision. Examples: "Do you want to brush your teeth before your story, or after?" "Do you want to make your bed before you have breakfast, or after?" In both examples, although they may sound trivial, there is a lot of learning about decision making going on.

For example, by stating "This is your decision to make," it is clear to both the parent and the child that the child is responsible for the final decision within the boundaries established by the parent: your teeth will be brushed; you will make your bed. These types of decisions are typically easier for children to make because they are about tasks and sequences of events. Any attempts by the child to redefine the options, e.g., "But I don't want to make my bed," are quickly dealt with by simply saying, "We're way past that. Your decision is about when you will do it."

Trickier decisions left to the child often arise when people are involved, e.g., "Do you want to invite Billy or Sally over to play?" "You have two birthday parties at the same time. Which one will you attend?" In these examples, the child may need the parent to help him/her figure out the various options and alternatives to get to the point where the child feels ready to make the final decision. The child may want the parent to make the decision, but the parent should resist taking on decisions that the child should be assuming.

Then there are those decisions that rightfully should be made by the parent. This category of decisions should be the easiest to deal with, but often end up being the most difficult because many parents are uncomfortable or fearful of saying no to their kids, and/or their kids have learned how to brow beat their parents until they get their way. Part of the supporting language for these kinds of decisions to be made by the parent is to say, "This is not negotiable," or "This is my decision—it is final, and I am not open to discussion or influence." If the parent doesn't waffle, the focus then shifts to helping the child deal with the decision that has been made on his/her behalf.

Whether the child or the parent gets to make which final decision will vary from one family to another. Let's take the example of the ten-year-old who wants to go to overnight camp. In one family, the parents may totally leave that decision up to the child. Another set of parents may decree there will be no overnight camp until the child is 13 or older. And finally, other parents may say, "We'll make the final decision, but here's your chance to make your case." After the child has had negotiated, persuaded, and/or influenced, the parent needs to say, "Okay, I've heard your reasons for your position. Here's what I've decided." It is important the child understands that the window for giving his/her input is closed. Otherwise, the child may persist in "making his case" and the parent feels badgered.

Back to your sister-in-law and her feeling guilty about a decision she and her husband have made. As parents, Barbara and her husband have rightfully and appropriately made the decision that Catherine will be joining her sister at Private School B next year. Decision made. Now Barbara and her husband's discussions with Catherine need to be about the inevitable changes that are a natural part of life, the parents sharing their experiences of how they have dealt with various changes in their lives, and what might be done to help make the transition from one school to another easier for Catherine.

However, before they have this discussion with Catherine, I would suggest that Barbara, her husband, and both girls sit down and review how the three different types of final decisions are made in their family, e.g., some by the kids themselves, some by the parents, and others by the parents with input from the kids. Earlier is better, but it is never too late to come together so the parents can help their children understand how decision making works in their family.

{Chapter 14}

I Am Heartsick with Guilt: My Grandson Got Seriously Burned While in My Charge

Dear Gramma Karen,

I am the grandfather of a 16-month-old boy, Donald. For financial reasons Donald and his parents live with my wife and me; they have lived with us since before Donald was born. Last week while I was keeping an eye on him, he pulled my steaming bowl of soup onto himself. My wife and I rushed him to the hospital where he was treated for serious burns. He was in the intensive care/burn unit at a local pediatric hospital for several days before he was discharged.

Arrangements were made by our daughter-in-law to temporarily move into her parents' home so that Donald could heal, which he is doing nicely. His physicians are very optimistic that he will make a full recovery with no scarring. As you can imagine, I am dealing with a lot of guilt. I keep reminding myself that I did not intentionally hurt him and that he will be okay. I have a good therapist who is helping me as well.

A few days ago I went to visit Donald at his other grandparents' house. The minute he saw me he ran to a corner and began shaking his head and crying "No!" He would not come near me. I left crying.

Now I am told his mother does not intend on moving back into our home until he is fully healed: three to six months. All along our daughter-in-law has reassured me that she does not blame me, but now she won't even bring Donald to our house, and I certainly cannot go back to the other grandparents' house.

Here is my question: How do I begin to rebuild this relationship with my grandson? Is there a group of guilty grandparents out there that I can turn to? I feel helpless. Any suggestions would be appreciated.

Although I do not know the number of grandparents who have direct experience with your tragic situation, I do know that being the caretaker when a grandchild gets hurt is something every grandparent thinks about, even obsesses about. I am confident that I speak for all grandparents when I reference the song "My Heart Goes Out to You."

The guilt you feel is inevitable, at least initially. I say "initially" because dealing with guilt has five stages before it can be accompanied or replaced by a sense of inner peace: (1) feelings of disappointment/anger/sorrow because of one's own behavior; (2) acceptance of one's role in the guilt-provoking situation; (3) a commitment to learn from the situation and to move forward in positive ways; (4) self forgiveness; (5) reaching out to make restitution with those we've hurt by our actions.

I think dealing with these five stages is complicated for you by the mixed messages your daughter-in-law seems to be giving. She tells you she does not blame you for Donald's accident. However, her actions contradict her words:

• Moving Donald out of your home, which was his home, too,

is suggesting that your home is not a safe place.

- Taking Donald to the other grandparents to heal could mean that she doesn't think you and your wife are up to the task.
- By not insisting you visit at the other grandparents' home, you are being marginalized.

I suggest your daughter-in-law's actions, and I assume they are supported by your son, are making it harder for you to rebuild your relationship with your grandson because it appears that at least right now she's not really committed to you having the relationship with Donald that you had prior to the accident. I think she would have behaved differently if she did not blame you, either consciously or unconsciously, for Donald's accident. Donald would still be living in your home with you, your wife, your son, and daughter-in-law. The other grandparents would be visiting frequently, with all of you working together to help Donald with his recovery in his usual environment.

These actions would have signaled an acceptance that terrible things, like this accident, sometimes happen in life. People make mistakes, such as leaving hot soup within a baby's reach, but when the person making the mistake is loved and forgiven, family members all pull together to help everyone heal, including the person who made the mistake and is suffering from guilt. The goal is to reestablish normalcy for Donald as quickly as possible. If your son and daughter-in-law want to redefine what normalcy for Donald is going to be in the future, that is certainly their prerogative and you will have to abide by whatever they decide. However, in fairness to you and your wife, you need to know what your role is to be in Donald's future.

I am glad that you have a good therapist because he or she could be instrumental in helping all of you clarify your feelings, share them and make sure everyone's feelings and actions are not working at cross purposes to Donald's detriment. I am not saying your daughter-in-law should or should not blame you for what happened: She's feeling what she's feeling. I am saying that perhaps your therapist could bring you all together to help you better understand what each of you is feeling, how these feelings are getting translated into actions, and what the implications are for Donald. At the very least your therapist could facilitate a discussion of your daughter-in-law's mixed messages.

Most important, because Donald is at an age where he is learning to read others' emotions and feelings, all the critical people in his life must act in ways that do not cause him to be scared, confused, and fearful. The good thing about Donald being so young is that over time the memories of this tragic accident will fade, including the fact that you were there when it happened, especially if he consistently sees his parents and his other grandparents being welcoming of you and treating you with warmth and love.

If your son and daughter-in-law are unwilling to meet with you and your therapist, perhaps over time, as Donald continues to improve, they will be more receptive to your participation in family gatherings and will eventually move back into your home. Meanwhile, your phone calls and cards will reassure them that you care about them, you miss them, and that you are willing to do whatever they ask of you so you can spend time with your grandson.

You said it would be of comfort to you if other grandparents who have had similar experiences would share them with you. I will forward you responses from my readers.

In closing, I know I am not alone in sending Donald warmest wishes for a speedy and complete recovery.

{Readers' Responses}

Many readers responded with an outpouring of empathy, encouragement, and sharing of their own experiences. The responses seemed to reflect three major themes, with the first theme along the lines of the phrase made famous in 1510 by John Bradford, who served Henry VIII of England, as he watched some prisoners being lead away to be executed: "There, but for the grace of God, go I."

Parents and grandparents alike expressed great empathy for Donald's grandfather as they shared the details of their own close calls when they were taking care of children or grandchildren. They recall with horror, even years later, what could have happened. One grandparent said, *"Any parent or grandparent who cannot relate to what happened to Donald and his grandfather is either unbelievably lucky or delusional."*

A second theme emerging from readers' responses referenced the idiom "in the blink of an eye." That is, events involving children and grandchildren happening so fast, literally in the time it takes to blink an eye (between 300-400 milliseconds, or 1/3 of a second, to be exact). One grandmother wrote: *"Several years ago when I was watching my then-14-month-old granddaughter in the bathtub, I left her for no more than a few seconds while I ran and turned down the stove. In those few seconds she pulled a piece off a plastic toy, put it in her mouth and was choking. Fortunately, I was able to get it out of her mouth. I know what Donald's grandfather is going through. Yes, he should have put the bowl of soup in a safer place. He made a mistake. I should not have left my granddaughter unattended. I made a mistake."*

A young mom writes: *"I was at the playground with my toddler. I was watching him when all of a sudden he was wandering into the path of a swing with a big kid on it coming right at him. I scooped him out of the way, but if I had delayed even a second later... I cannot even bear to think about it. And I was watching his every move! Things can happen so fast. We can only do the best we can do. I think about this incident whenever I am tempted to take my eyes off him. No more 'just one quick text' for me when I'm watching him."*

A third discernible theme was a bit of a surprise. Many parents and grandparents who had brushes with potential accidents when they were taking care of their children or grandchildren said they never discussed them with anyone! They were fearful other family members would judge them to be negligent or irresponsible. The grandparents in particular were afraid the young parents would not trust them to be with the grandchildren alone.

Many described how they were able to rechannel their guilt constructively by treating their close calls as a wake-up call: They vowed to pay closer attention and be more mindful when they were in charge of their children or grandchildren. One parent wrote that what happened to Donald prompted her to clean out her garage as it is full of stuff like saws and rakes that could injure her own and the neighborhood kids when they're getting bikes and toys. She said she would never forgive herself if her laziness was the reason a child got injured.

With regard to Donald's grandfather asking about support from other grandparents dealing with similar guilt, one reader wrote: *"My guess is that some real support may come from outside the family. He might go for support to a minister or rabbi, check his church for general support groups, or even go to a group that is not designed for his situation—he will find kindness and forgiveness waiting for him. . . . Please remind this grandfather that none of us goes through life without hurting someone else in some way."* Another reader suggests AARP's Foundation GrandCare Support Locator (http:// www.giclocalsupport.org/pages/gic_db_home.cfm). Although this locator focuses primarily on visitation issues, it does provide information for grandparents who want to connect to support groups for other issues. It could be a starting point.

Another reader suggests that Donald's father not put time and effort into trying to find other "guilty" grandparents because everyone's experience and family relationships are different. Yes, he may find comfort in talking with grandparents who were eventually forgiven, but he may also talk with grandparents who were never forgiven and this will only make him feel worse.

I am pleased to close this column with an update from Donald's grandfather: *"Donald continues to improve both physically and emotionally . . . They have all moved back into our home. We (my wife, son, and daughter-in-law) speak openly about what happened and about our feelings. I really thought that I would want to avoid speaking with any family member of the event, but I have found a tremendous sense of comfort in being open and honest about everything. It turns out that I was really the only one blaming me.*

"As for my relationship with Donald, he is still a bit apprehensive with me. If I attempt to pick him up or hold his hand, he pulls away. However, if I allow him to approach me to read a book or sit beside me at a meal, he'll do so without trepidation, as long as it is on his terms. This is just fine with me, and I am grateful.

"Time is definitely healing. What remains is a tremendous sense of gratitude, a newfound closeness within our family, and a heightened sense of awareness regarding safety in our home.

"I am overwhelmed with gratitude and I feel the warmth of your readers' sympathy and empathy."

{Chapter 15}

I Don't Want My Mother-in-Law to Babysit

Dear Dr. Gramma Karen:

Both my husband and I work full time. We used to have our three-year-old daughter Alice in a day-care program that she really loved going to and we felt was good for her. However, when my mother-in-law had a forced retirement a couple of months ago and said that she'd like to be Alice's full-time babysitter, we took her out of the program. We thought it would be a good thing to do because my mother-in-law wouldn't charge us to sit for Alice and we are saving up for a house.

This has been a mistake. As it turns out, although my mother-in-law adores Alice and takes good care of her, she doesn't really interact with her in stimulating ways, e.g., puzzles, books, creative play, helping her with coloring and basic writing, all things Alice was doing in day care. I've asked my mother-in-law to do more of these activities and cut down on the TV time, but things have not really changed. My husband agrees with me, but is afraid of hurting his mother's feelings. I don't want to let this continue because I think Alice would be learning more back in day care.

Your husband is your immediate challenge, not your

mother-in-law (MIL), but we'll discuss that in a moment. First, the fact that your MIL was forced to retire, often a traumatizing experience resulting in hasty and emotionally-driven decisions, may mean she never had a chance to plan and prepare for her retirement. She may have rushed into offering to be Alice's full-time sitter so she could feel needed and have something purposeful to do.

As often happens, you and your husband got pulled into your mother-in-law's circumstances, and in retrospect, and understandably, you made a hasty decision that you now regret. You saw a way to help your MIL deal with her forced retirement, while at the same helping you save some money. It all made sense at the time, but the current situation is that your husband's heart is in the right place in not wanting to hurt your MIL's feelings, but sparing her feelings is negatively impacting what you both want for Alice.

You need to help your husband do some shifting of priorities. Right now it seems he is overly focused on not hurting his mother's feelings, but this is at the expense of doing what you've both decided is best for Alice. At this point you have probably stated and restated to your husband several times the changes needed. You're probably in a loop: You express, your husband nods in agreement, and nothing changes. You need to break this loop.

The first thing you might do is work with your husband in scripting a message for your MIL, for example, something along the lines of: "Mom, we've made a decision we want to share with you. First we want to thank you for taking such good care of Alice these past few months. You and Alice had some special time together and you helped us add to our fund for a down payment on a house. You are such a great help. Thank you!

"We've decided to put Alice in her day-care program as

we feel she's at a good age now to really benefit educationally and socially. What we want to talk with you about is that we're hoping you'll continue to be available to help us out, occasionally doing drop offs and pickups and maybe the two of you spending one afternoon a week together. We want to see what might work for you. Again, we can't thank you enough for your help."

You'll notice that there are no apologies in the suggested message, as there is nothing you need to apologize for; you are just exercising your parental responsibilities. Also, you are making it clear that your MIL's involvement has been a big help, you're very grateful, and that you want to explore mutually beneficial ways for her to stay involved, if this is of interest to her. She may now have some other ideas on how she wants to spend her time.

I suggest your husband needs to take the lead giving your MIL this message, to make it clear that you and your husband are aligned on this. You and your husband can figure out whether your husband first e-mails the message to your MIL and then you both discuss it with her, or if you and your husband together deliver it to her in person.

Having a scripted message may help your husband act on what the two of you have decided. If he's still hesitant, you may think about involving a third party so your husband can hear from someone, other than you, that he needs to shift his priorities. This third party should be someone you both respect, e.g., family member, a friend, Alice's pediatrician, your own physician(s), a family counselor or practitioner, a colleague, someone from Alice's program.

This approach of using a scripted message may help your husband feel more comfortable in removing his mom from full-time babysitting, while at the same time reassuring him that being both a great dad and a loving son are not mutually exclusive!

PART 3

Assumptions and Expectations
Avoiding Disappointment

{Chapter 16}

My Mother-in-Law's Lack of Support Angers Me

Dear Dr. Gramma Karen:

I want to get rid of the anger and bitterness I feel towards my mother-in-law. She lives 20 minutes away, but doesn't ever offer to come by to help or just to see her three-year-old grandson. She is a very socially active woman with golf, luncheons, and friends. She has three older grandchildren from her other son and seems to have given them a lot of attention. She expects us to come over to her home on weekends, which are busy for us, to see her for coffee, not for dinner. She is nice when we're there visiting.

Both my husband and I thought she would have been more supportive. My husband does not want to confront her because he feels that he has asked her to come around and visit in his own way. Also, there are some additional hurts that resulted when my husband worked in the family-owned business my MIL and her deceased husband owned.

I spend a great deal of time worrying about this and what we have done wrong. It's causing stress in our marriage. I don't want our son to pick up on all this. Advice, please!

When you say both you and your husband thought your mother-in-law (MIL) "would have been more supportive," you've made some assumptions about how you think she should act and behave as a grandmother. Actor Henry Winkler's famous quote, "Assumptions are the termites of relationships," seems appropriate in your situation. As long as you hold on to your miscommunicated or never-communicated expectations about how your MIL should act as a grandmother, the anger and bitterness you feel towards her will continue to gnaw. If your MIL senses your anger and frustration with her, she may feel tense and uncomfortable around you and want to limit her interactions.

Before we talk about how you might progress, one point: It is easy in hindsight to say that the ideal time to work out the assumptions and expectations for how you want grandparents to fulfill their roles is before the first grandchild arrives or to address them head on as they arise. The fact that your son is three suggests those windows of opportunities for discussing your assumptions have already passed. To revisit them now would probably result in a destructive emotional torrent that does more harm than good and has the potential to damage relationships beyond repair. Also, as you indicate, there are other factors in play around the family business that complicate the relationships, e.g., history and dynamics.

So, here are some things you can do to maintain a cordial relationship with your MIL that do not require bringing up old hurts, frustrations, and disappointments. Since your MIL does want you to visit in her home on weekends for coffee, and you say these visits are pleasant, then that is what you can do: Let go of all your old assumptions and expectations and plan visits that are in response to her invitations. Over time, you may find her more responsive to your reaching out.

In short, I'm suggesting a new playbill for you. Drop the current drama that focuses on your constant disappointment and hurt resulting from your assumptions about how your MIL should behave, and shift to a focus on the relationship between your son and your MIL. You need to become a supporting actor in which your role is to make sure your son gets to spend as much time as possible with his grandmother, even if it requires inconvenience to you and your husband. In your new supporting role I suggest you adopt a mantra of "I need to be cordial and pleasant, cordial and pleasant, cordial and pleasant" to remind you of what's really important. Instead of wishing your MIL were different and hoping she'll change, I'm suggesting you make some changes—changes that have a far better chance of getting rid of your anger and bitterness, and can help your MIL and son have a nice relationship.

{Chapter 17}

I Don't Want My Husband's Illiterate Stepmother to Babysit

Dear Dr. Gramma Karen:

My wonderful mother-in-law passed away three years ago. Last year my father-in-law, Edward, a successful, and now-retired cardiologist, married Sally, a widow with grown children and two grandchildren. From the bits and pieces I've put together, Sally grew up in a very poor, rural family in a southern state. Apparently her first husband was a good provider, working for a utility company; their kids always speak well of him and Sally. Edward met Sally at a grief counseling group.

Although Sally is always pleasant to be around, she is not what you'd expect for a doctor's wife. In fact, I think Sally is illiterate. I say this because whenever anything requires reading, I've noticed that Edward does it for her, e.g., a menu, shopping list, what movies are playing, texts. Also, they are always telling us about the books on tape they listen to together. Sally does not drive; she never has.

This is the situation: I am pregnant with our first child, and because I think Sally is illiterate, I do not want her babysitting, something she and Edward have said repeatedly they are looking forward to doing for us. Something could happen to the baby if a situation required Sally to read and she is not able to. I want to say something to them, but my husband disagrees. What do you think?

You say your deceased mother-in-law was wonderful (and I truly am sorry for your loss). Sally, however, seems to be a long way from wonderful in your estimation. In fact, she seems to be a disappointment to you. Blending new members into a family is often difficult, and based on your description of your situation, I think it is accurate to say you are less than enthusiastic of Edward's choice of Sally. You say "she is not what you'd expect for a doctor's wife," and although you do not elaborate, it seems she falls short of some expectations you have for what constitutes an acceptable "doctor's wife." So, through no fault of Sally's, the chances of the two of you building a good relationship are minimized from the get-go, unless you are willing to make some changes.

Let's start with your suspicion that Sally is illiterate. Statistically, Sally has an almost 50-50 chance of being a nonreader or someone who faces reading challenges. According to the U.S. Department of Education, National Center for Education Statistics (http://www.national-coalition-literacy.org/litfacts.html), one in seven American adults lacks sufficient reading skills. Specifically, in the adult American population:

- 21 to 23 percent (40 to 44 million) are totally or functionally illiterate.
- 26 percent (50 million) are marginally illiterate.
- 52 percent (100 million) are fully literate.

Sadly, for all our many national strengths, 14 countries rank higher than the U.S. on reading abilities.

So, yes, reading and computational skills for Sally may be minimal or nonexistent; you're not sure. But what you can be sure about is the fact that she has proven herself a capable wife, mother, and grandmother. Sally and Edward are two people who met and bonded while trying to deal with the loss of their respective spouses. They decided to build a life together. It appears they spend a lot of time together, and are doing so by choice. It could very well be that Edward enjoys taking the lead in the activities they do together, including reading and going over lists. Sally, having raised two kids and all that involves, may thoroughly enjoy being fussed over by Edward.

The point is that you don't have any deep insight into the dynamics, details, and nuances of their relationship. A related point is that they determine what they wish to share with you about themselves as individuals and as a couple. For you to suggest to Sally that she is illiterate would be incredibly inappropriate and intrusive, certain to cause humiliation and embarrassment, perhaps even anger and estrangement. To do so under the pretext that your baby's safety may be at risk feels to me a bit of a stretch. My advice is that you work on feeling grateful that you have in-laws who are excited about being your baby's grandparents and are already letting you know they want to be involved to help you and your husband after the baby arrives.

The truth of the matter is that anyone who is going to be a caretaker for your baby has to earn your trust, and as first-time parents, you and your husband will be understandably extra cautious and anxious about leaving your child with someone else. This includes your parents, siblings, close friends, nannies, and babysitters, as well as Edward and Sally. They all will need you and your husband to be clear with them about their responsibilities in taking care of your baby. They will be left in charge of your child with increasing frequency and duration as they gain your trust.

I'll close by suggesting that I am not sure the primary issue is about Sally's literacy, or lack thereof. Rather, what may be troubling you may have more to do with the death of your mother-in-law, how much you miss her, and the difficulty you may be having in accepting how Edward has been able to live his life apparently so happily with someone else. If you focus more on trying to be happy that Edward and Sally have each other, you may find that your heart lightens and you get great comfort in knowing your baby will have loving and available grandparents.

If you work now on being a loving and supportive daughter-in-law, it will make it easier to discuss any future caretaking concerns you have with Edward and Sally because you will raise your concerns within the context of strong and caring relationships.

{Chapter 18}

I Find It Difficult to Stay Overnight at My In-Laws' House

Dear Dr. Gramma Karen:

I feel really disappointed that my in-laws haven't made it easier for us to stay at their house with our 14-month-old daughter. They have yet to provide anything, such as a porta-crib, toys, or books. We'd like to visit them more, but we always have to schlep so much stuff.

They also don't like or support our routine, and if we try to suggest or change something, it is met with resistance. For example, when we told them that it's hard for our daughter to nap during the day because there's no way to make the room dark, they responded by saying, "She will have to learn to sleep in the daylight at some point." Another example: my father-in-law thunders up the uncarpeted stairs and will not take off his shoes or walk up the stairs, even though he often wakes the baby, because, he said, "It's what I like to do."

Visiting my parents is so much easier because they've equipped their home for us. Last spring my in-laws had hurt feelings when my parents babysat our daughter for a weekend. We tried to explain why it was much easier to take her to my parents, but nothing changed or has been discussed since. We otherwise enjoy visiting them and they love having us. We feel very welcome and they love getting to see their

*granddaughter. My husband feels the same way as I do. We're just
not sure what to do.*

I get the sense that as much as your in-laws love being
around you, your husband, and your daughter, it is out of their
comfort zone when you are actually living in their space. Hence,
I differentiate between spending time with them—which seems
to be enjoyable for everyone—and staying with them—not so
enjoyable.

It sounds like you've been forthright and kind in letting
them know what will work best for you, yet nothing has changed.
Based on the resistance you've experienced with the bright room
and the clomping shoes, it seems there is a bit of an edge to their
responses. Only you can determine if this possibility applies, but
many grandparents are confused, sometimes even annoyed, by their
adult children's childrearing practices. Some grandparents feel their
grandchildren are being overly indulged and need to be toughened
up ("She will have to learn to sleep in the daylight at some point"),
and/or feel their grandchildren need to learn that everything doesn't
always revolve around them ("It's what I like to do").

What to do? You've asked for some consideration and
accommodation and it doesn't seem to be forthcoming, so perhaps
when you plan visits with them in their home, you do not stay over.
If feasible, you may plan day trips. Or you may want to stay in a
hotel or motel, both of which typically have both the equipment
you need and dark closets large enough for a porta-crib.

If your in-laws express disappointment that you aren't
staying with them, you can explain, again, that it's easier for you
in a hotel where everything you need for staying over is more

readily available. If you're staying with them and you have to interrupt your visit to take your daughter back to the motel for a nap, you can explain, again, and always nicely, that she needs a dark and quiet place to nap. If your budget is tight, when they ask what they can get you for your birthday, tell them a night or two in a hotel or motel near them would be the perfect gift so you can visit with them.

For you and other young parents experiencing your situation, it might be that the grandparents have become very set in their ways and routines and find it difficult to change. Or, they might feel you're in their home, and it's up to you to bring whatever you need, as their days of buying and maintaining baby stuff are behind them. For other grandparents who are on a strict budget, outfitting their homes may seem like a burdensome expense, in which case you might be able to purchase the basics you need and leave them at their home to cut down on your packing and schlepping.

It is unfortunate that your in-laws don't see that they cannot have it both ways. On the one hand, they are hurt that your daughter got to stay with the other grandparents, but on the other hand, when you explained why, they did not step it up and meet your clearly-explained needs.

The good news about your situation is that you, your husband, and your daughter feel welcome and have a good time when you're together, so I suggest you focus on spending time with your in-laws in their home, but not stay over with them right now while they are unable or unwilling to accommodate your family. As your daughter gets older and needs less of what is currently lacking, you may find staying with your in-laws, with or without you and your husband present, becomes easier for all of you.

For the time being, if you have the space and motivation, the simplest solution might be for them to come and visit you, and you can explain it's just easier on all of you while your daughter is so young.

{Chapter 19}

My Resentment Is Growing as My Son's Family Temporarily Lives with Us

Dear Dr. Gramma Karen:

Our son Danny and his wife Cheryl have two children, four-year-old Gretchen and two-year-old Nate. When Danny and his family, who live in another state, decided to build a new home, he called and said they needed to live with us for five months while their new home is being built.

We are now into the second month and my husband and I are at our wits' end. We are both retired, used to a nice routine of enjoying some separate activities and doing other things together. Before Danny and his family moved in, our home was quiet and relaxed.

Both Danny and Cheryl have jobs they can do by computer. They've taken over my sewing room and made it into their joint office. They work all day and expect my husband and me to take care of the kids. This is not really what we want to be doing, but we thought we could do it for five months to help them out. The main problem is Gretchen. She is whiny, demanding, uncooperative, and fresh. Her parents also find her difficult to manage, but they shrug off her behavior and say she's just going through a stage.

My husband and I are exhausted and not sure we can do this for another three months (and the construction of their new house seems to be a bit behind in schedule). We don't want to start any kind of a family feud. Do you have any advice for us?

Your current situation of multiple generations living together is not unique. In fact, you are among the more than 51.4 million Americans of all ages—or about one in six—living in a multigenerational household. This number represents a more than 10 percent increase since the start of the Great Recession in 2007. Most multigenerational families are together because of financial considerations, while others, such as yours, choose to live together for other reasons. Not surprising, in a recent Harris Poll sponsored by Generations United (http://www.gu.org/LinkClick.aspx?file ticket=QWOTaluHxPk%3d&tabid=157&mid=606), 78 percent agreed that "At times, my family's multigenerational arrangement can contribute to stress among family members."

You attribute the main source of stress to your four-year-old granddaughter Gretchen. However, as difficult as interacting with Gretchen is for you, your husband, and her parents, I suggest that she is a symptom of the real problem, not the source. The main problem you and many other multigenerational families face is that you never put in place a plan once it was agreed to share living space. It is too easy to assume that things will just work themselves out, but, as you have learned, just hoping and leaving things to chance often does not work.

What's required is A Plan for Living Together, including guidelines and discussion points. In this way erroneous assumptions can be minimized and realistic and agreed-upon expectations can be maximized. Although you are already two months into your young family living with you, it is still not too late for you to initiate a plan. You and your husband can explain to Danny and Cheryl that you feel a discussion and a plan will help ensure the next few months are as comfortable and stress-free as possible for everyone.

Below is a sample of such a plan. (Next to some of the discussion points I have included parenthetical comments specifically for you and your family.)

A Plan for Multigenerational Families Temporarily Living Together

Guidelines
- The plan should be in writing.
- The plan should be discussed and agreements reached before anyone actually moves in.
- When living together, there should be a weekly family meeting to review what's working well with the plan, what is not working so well, and what needs to be done to address various issues and concerns.
- Family members moving in must respect and give top priority to the requests and preferences of the "host" family members.

Discussion Points
1. Understand and discuss the reasons why family members are moving in and why the host family is agreeing to this arrangement. (I suspect that you and your husband thought you were being asked just to provide a temporary place for

Danny and his family to live, but it sounds like Danny and Cheryl assumed that you would also be full-time caretakers for their children. Because this was not clarified, there was no discussion about the possibility of hiring a nanny for the children and/or enrolling them in any kind of a day-care or nursery program.)

2. **Agree to a specific timeline for family members to move in, and when possible, to move out.** (If there are long-term problems with the construction of the new home, you may want to discuss the possibility of Danny and his family moving into a furnished apartment. They may be agreeable, as it is probably difficult for them living in "your" space.)

3. **Negotiate changes in furnishings, layout, and use of space.** (Granted, Danny and Cheryl need work space, and it may be acceptable to you to give up your sewing room, but these kinds of changes need to be discussed up front. You may have preferred they take over the basement, or some other space in the house, or perhaps that they rent a small office nearby. Another important area for discussion is where the children's clothes, toys, and equipment will be kept.)

4. **Discuss financial considerations and expectations.** (This is especially important if you and/or Danny and Cheryl are on a tight budget.)

5. **Host family members need to define areas of their space and/or aspects of their schedules, routines, and preferences they do not wish to change.** (You and your husband may have activities, classes or social engagements that you are unwilling to give up. These need to be posted on a central calendar making it known when you are available and when you are unavailable.)

6. **Family members moving in need to make known their preferences,**

needs, and wishes regarding space in the home, as well as their preferred schedules and routines. (Although Danny and Cheryl should be trying to accommodate you and your husband's schedules and routines, they, too, should be clear about ways in which they would appreciate you accommodating them, if possible. For example, they may need the kitchen at specific times to keep their kids on a schedule.)

7. **All family members must be clear as to the help they would like from all the other family members.** (For example, if Danny and Cheryl are hoping you can take the children to swim lessons and/or other activities while they are working, you and your husband need to be clear about how much time you will reserve for these kinds of activities with the grandchildren and post a schedule of your availability. Danny and Cheryl need to be able to count on you.)

8. **Behavioral expectations for all parties need to be discussed.** (For example, if you are watching Gretchen and she is being unruly and fresh, Danny and Cheryl need to know that you may want to turn her over to them, even if they are working.)

This plan is offered as an example of format and content, but you, your husband, Danny, and Cheryl have to customize it for your particular circumstances. The point of the plan is to provide a vehicle for talking about the specifics of what needs to happen to lessen conflicts and to make sure issues are addressed in a timely manner, e.g., the weekly family meeting.

Yes, Danny, Cheryl, and your grandchildren are family, but they are also "guests" in your home. You and your husband need to take control of your lives and your space and work out together with Danny and Cheryl how to live together comfortably. Otherwise, you will likely find yourselves feeling resentful, taken advantage of, exhausted, and unable to enjoy this very special time with your grandchildren.

{Chapter 20}

I Don't Want to Babysit My Grandchildren Any Longer

Dear Dr. Gramma Karen:

I babysit for my two granddaughters and I don't want to do it any longer. You'll probably say, "So then, stop already," but it's not that simple.

When my deceased husband and I were raising our two daughters, I worked full time as an attorney in a prestigious law firm. I loved my job and I made good money that helped pay for our family's very nice lifestyle. However, my job meant I missed a lot of my daughters' sports and extra-curricular activities.

When my daughter Fiona's first daughter was born four years ago, I told Fiona that I wanted to make up for being an absentee mother when she was growing up, and that I would be available in any way she needed me with her children. Long and short is that I have become a full-time nanny for Fiona's two daughters, Hannah, 4, and Tammy, 2. I love my two granddaughters but my whole life revolves around taking care of them. When I told Fiona I didn't want to do it any longer, she made me feel guilty when she reminded me that I had promised to make up for being an absentee mother. I made a commitment and I guess I have to honor it. Do you agree?

You say your daughter made you feel guilty, so let's start with this question: Is guilt a friend or foe? Well, it depends. In general, guilt acts as a moral compass, alerting us that we're disappointed in ourselves, that is, we've let ourselves and/or others down. Psychologists talk about two main forms of guilt—constructive ("good guilt") and destructive ("bad guilt"). Guilt can be constructive when it results in our doing some soul searching, owning our mistakes and misdeeds, and making changes to keep us on the right path to be the person we want to be. Constructive guilt is healthy and productive and pushes us to make our lives better by either prompting us to do something or to stop doing something.

Destructive guilt, however, is unhealthy, unproductive, and can be debilitating. It can weaken or prevent our resolve to do better, to be better. It can render us stuck, emotionally immobilized, unable to learn, change, and move forward. It can leave us feeling embarrassed and/or ashamed; it can prevent us from acting deliberatively and decisively to strive to be our better selves. Destructive guilt can make us vulnerable to being controlled and manipulated by others.

First, I want to suggest that it is unfortunate that you use the term "working mom" interchangeably with "absentee mom." Yes, you were a working mother. You had a job and a paycheck that you put towards taking care of your family. And yes, as a working mom, you made certain sacrifices to keep that paycheck coming in. Many working moms feel constructive guilt and deal with it by spending more time with their children on weekends to compensate for spending less time with them on weekdays.

However, describing yourself as an absentee mom suggests someone who has checked out, not doing proper mothering, went AWOL (absent without leave). This is a self-image that can lead to destructive guilt. So my suggestion is that you think of your former self as a working mom, and not as an absentee mom, a notion that suggests you were an inadequate mom and now you are obligated to make it up to your daughter by being an enslaved grandmother.

When you say, "Fiona made me feel guilty," I want to suggest that it is more accurate to say, "I let Fiona make me feel guilty." Both you and Fiona, either wittingly or unwittingly, have been complicit in keeping you mired in destructive guilt. There's been a real gain for Fiona: She gets loving and immediate quality care for her daughters whenever she needs it. There's been a perceived gain for you: You get to feel you're making amends for something bad you did many years ago. I say perceived gain for you because the problem is you never did anything bad. The result is that you unnecessarily indentured yourself, but the good news is that you can un-indenture yourself. It really is that simple once you decide to throw off the yoke of destructive guilt.

When you're ready, you can tell Fiona that you want to give her some lead time to make other arrangements because you're making some changes in your life and you won't be available to take care of your granddaughters as you have been doing. You've decided to, for example, do some traveling, take some courses, do some volunteer work, go hang gliding, take some time to figure out what kinds of new things you want to do. Will Fiona be pleased and support your decision? Probably not, at least initially, but over time you can hope she adjusts. Will she try to use guilt again to change your mind? Maybe, but it won't work anymore because you're out of the destructive guilt game! In fairness to both you and your daughter, this time around you need to be clear about what you will and will not do with regard to your time with your granddaughters.

Now that you won't be spending as much time taking care of Hannah and Tammy, be sure to talk with them so they understand that they haven't done anything wrong. Explain to them that you love, love, love them and you'll always treasure the special time you've had with them taking care of them, but now it's time for you to branch out and do some other things. Explain that you'll still be spending special time with them, but in different ways.

{Chapter 21}

My Mother-in-Law Is a Liar

Dear Dr. Gramma Karen:

My husband and I have had it with his mother, Norma. She is a liar, claiming she doesn't smoke anymore, but we can smell smoke on both her and Bethany, our one-year-old daughter, after they've been together. Also, there have been times when we come home to open windows and whiffs of cigarette smoke in the air.

Norma doesn't live near us, but she comes to visit every couple of months and stays for a few days. She is great with Bethany and loves spending time with her, taking her for walks, hanging out at the playground, and playing with her in the apartment. My husband and I both work, so when Norma is here, we give our sitter time off because Norma likes her special time with Bethany.

My husband is ready to tell Norma that he can't abide her lying anymore, and she can just forget about visiting until she can prove to us, with a blood test or some other foolproof method, that she really has given up smoking. Do you have any ideas?

"My mother-in-law is a liar." Wow! Harsh. In order to fairly and calmly look at some possible options, let's reframe this characterization of Norma as a liar to say instead, "My mother-in-law is a nicotine addict and she lies to us to cover up her addiction." Many smokers, because they have difficulty freeing themselves from their addiction, tell lies about their nicotine addiction—they are embarrassed and ashamed, they often feel like a failure and a loser. Viewing her as having a serious physiological and psychological addiction, rather than a personality disorder, is not to excuse Norma, but understanding her behaviors may help you and your husband make good decisions about how best to deal with her. I see three options.

One option is to follow through on your husband's inclination to sever all ties with Norma until she can produce definitive proof that she is no longer a smoker. The downside of this approach is that it is based on a threat and its longer-term sustainability is poor. Smoking cessation studies are clear and consistent: Those who are able to remain non-smokers for at least a year are intrinsically motivated, meaning they want to quit smoking for themselves, not to please someone else or because they fear repercussions. Even when intrinsically motivated to stop smoking, success is hard won. National Institutes of Health (NIH) state that most successful smokers have tried to quit an average of seven times before finally being cigarette free. Although depriving Norma of seeing her granddaughter until she convinces you she is no longer smoking is an option, it is punitive and threat-based and chances for its success are short term, at best.

A variation of this option is to bombard Norma with all kinds of scary statistics—about 430,000 deaths per year are linked to cigarette smoking; in the United States, more people are killed each year by cigarettes than by alcohol, car crashes, suicide, AIDS, homicide, and illegal drugs combined—but like most smokers, Norma probably is already familiar with those numbers. If you share them with her because you're angry, you're back to scare tactics, and they don't have a great track record.

Another option is to stop being Norma's adversary. She already knows you're upset with her and you want her to stop, but nevertheless, she's still smoking and lying about it. Just accept her as a smoker and go from there. Tell her you love her, you're afraid her smoking is going to cause her serious health problems and may eventually kill her; let her know you've come to realize that she will quit smoking on her own when she's ready and you're not going to bug her about quitting anymore.

Assure her that you know how important her relationship with Bethany is to both of them and you want them to continue to spend time together. This said, tell her you're concerned about the secondhand smoke her smoking causes because you've learned secondhand smoke annually causes between 150,000 and 300,000 lower respiratory infections in children younger than 18 months, and results in 7,000 to 15,000 hospitalizations each year; secondhand smoke kills an estimated 50,000 Americans a year.

Further, you've learned that third-hand smoke, referred to as "the smoke that sticks around," is the residue that smoke leaves on furniture, carpets, walls, clothing, food, even in dust. It poses its own health hazards. Turning on a fan or opening a window does only a little to get rid of the penetrating odor and clinging compounds. Granted, the danger is certainly small compared to secondhand smoke, though the exposures are often longer. Still, no level of these hazardous compounds is safe, especially for children and infants, who are more vulnerable.

And finally, tell Norma that as long as she is a smoker, she needs to make certain commitments when she is around Bethany to ensure that her smoking is not jeopardizing Bethany's health. You understand that Norma currently cannot go long periods of time without smoking, so you've decided to have the babysitter around when Norma and Bethany are together. When Norma needs to smoke, the babysitter assumes care of Bethany. Most important, under no circumstances does Norma smoke anywhere near Bethany where secondhand or third-hand smoke, inside or outside the home, can be a factor.

Perhaps you will agree that the approach I am suggesting has several advantages, because it:

- Accepts Norma for what she is, an addicted smoker.
- Re-channels the anger, frustration, and disappointment you feel towards her.
- Makes it easier for Norma to talk about her addiction instead of trying to cover it up.
- Keeps Bethany (and you, too!) safe from Norma's second-hand and third-hand smoke.
- Preserves all the family relationships.

{Chapter 22}

I'm Very Hurt by Something My Daughter Said about Me

Dear Dr. Gramma Karen:

We live near our daughter Carly, her husband, and their two children, Mikey, who is five, and Julie, who is ten. We spend a lot of enjoyable time with their family, sometimes babysitting, sometimes just everybody being together.

A couple of weeks ago when the grandchildren were spending the weekend with us while their parents went on a mini-vacation, Mikey said, "Grandma, Mommy said you don't dress your age. What does that mean?" When Mikey said that, I took a deep breath and calmly told him that people have different ideas about what constitutes fashion, but the truth is that I was absolutely floored! I take great pride in my appearance. I go to the gym at least three times a week, I watch what I eat. I think I look pretty good for my age, and I try to dress with flair and style.

I thought I had a great relationship with Carly, but I am so hurt that she would say something so negative and hurtful about the way I dress. My husband thinks I am overreacting. I am not sure what I should do.

You deserve credit for being kind and sensitive in your response to Mikey by not reacting emotionally with him or doing anything to "punish the messenger." Sounds like he is an innocent player in this situation, as he was just repeating something he heard and didn't understand. So, what, if anything, might you say to your daughter?

Let's try a hypothetical situation: If your ten-year-old granddaughter Julie came to you and said, "Grandma, my feelings are hurt because one of my girlfriends said she doesn't like the way I dress," I suspect you would suggest that what is important, first and foremost, is that she needs to dress for herself—that is, in ways that help her feel good about herself (and are deemed appropriate by her parents, as she is, after all, only ten). Further, you would probably suggest to her that, in general, dressing to please others is ultimately a losing battle, because inevitably, some will like her choices and others will not. I say "in general" because there might be people whose approval is important.

This brings us back to your daughter saying something hurtful about the way you dress. You say you eat right, you regularly exercise, and you try to dress with "flair and style," all of which suggest strong, positive, and self-confident actions on your part. Here is the critical question you need to answer: Is it important to you that Carly approves of your fashion choices? If not, then there isn't any need to do or say anything.

However, the fact that you say your feelings are hurt suggests you do want Carly to approve of the way you dress. If so, then you have some options. For example, you can tell Carly you value her opinion and because you're thinking about making some wardrobe changes, you'd like her advice. However, a cardinal rule about asking for advice is that you have to be open to the possibility that the advice you get flies in the face of your self-image. In fact, if you want her candid comments you may have to emphasize that you're serious about making some changes and she needs to be forthright with you. If she tells you she thinks you should dress in ways that are more flattering and/or appropriate for you, then you have to listen and not become defensive. You need to ask for specific examples so you really understand her advice. She may make some suggestions that make sense to you.

Another option is for you to read some fashion books and articles on your own, or meet with a fashion or style consultant. (For example, if you Google "style or fashion consultants in Manhattan," you'll get several million hits!) Once you have some ideas, then you can approach your daughter and share with her some of the fashion tips and strategies you're thinking about and ask her what she thinks.

You'll notice in my suggestions that Mikey doesn't come into the discussion at all. This is about you, your daughter, and a comment she made. If you lead with "Mikey said . . . ," the focus is going to be on Mikey and his repeating something, and I don't think this is where the problem lies. Unless, what is really bothering you is that your daughter said something negative about you in front of Mikey or within his earshot. If this is the case, you may want to just let the whole matter go because you probably don't want to have a conversation with your daughter in which you try to tell her what she should and should not say about you in her own home.

Another possibility is that when you bring up the topic of your wardrobe, your daughter laughs and says Mikey told her what he repeated to you and she was wondering if his comment made an impact on you. If this is the case, you can brush it off, or you can let Carly know that your feelings were hurt. Carly may apologize if she hurt your feelings, but then again, there may be some substance to her comment that she will share with you, if you invite her to do so.

The fact that you feel you have a great relationship with your daughter suggests this one, isolated incident should be treated just as that—a one-off occurrence that can hopefully be easily addressed, if at all, and then forgotten. I think this is perhaps what your husband meant when he said you were overreacting.

{ Readers' Comments }

Dear Readers:

After reading my column, "My Grandson Repeated Something Hurtful My Daughter Said," several readers shared personal childhood stories about repeating something they overheard, some getting into trouble for doing so, others aware that they had somehow embarrassed their parents. I thank the reader who sent me the following reminder that kids are always listening—and what they hear, they just might repeat!

The Family Dinner Party (author unknown)

A friend hosted a dinner party for family far and wide
    and everyone
Was encouraged to bring all their children as well.

All during the sit-down dinner one four-year-old girl
Stared at the uncle sitting across from her.

The girl could hardly eat her food for staring.

The uncle checked his tie, felt his face for food, patted his hair in
Place but nothing stopped her from staring at him.

He tried his best to just ignore her but finally it was too much for
Him.

He finally asked her "Why are you staring at me?"

Everyone at the table had noticed her behavior and the
        table went
Quiet for her response.

The little girl said, "I just want to see how you drink like a fish."

{Chapter 23}

Please Help Take the Stress Out of Gift Giving

Dear Dr. Gramma Karen:

I want to suggest you do a column on gift giving. I ask because I listen to people at work and in the check-out lines in stores stressing out about this. For example, my co-workers, who are young parents, talk about their in-laws as being either cheapskates or extravagant. Then there is the topic of grandparents giving the grandchildren gifts that the parents have already said they don't want the kids to have, e.g., cellphones, video games.

I'm happy to say we've solved all this in my large family by doing a grab bag. Actually we do two grab bags, one for the adults and a second one for the children. Anyone who wants to participate puts their name in a hat. Names are drawn, and then, instead of buying gifts for 21 adults and 6 kids, one gift is purchased for the name drawn. (The parents of the kids in their grab bag buy the one gift for the child they drew.) The gifts are opened one at a time, and it's a lot of fun. We've done it this way for years. It's very stress free, except for the person who forgets whose name he/she drew; that's why one person needs to keep a master list.

It's amazing to me when I tell people about our family's grab bag, and everyone says, "What a great idea, I wish our family would do that," but it seems no one has the courage to approach the topic with their family members (who might even feel the same way!), so the frustration, time, and expense mount up year after year.

So, although I'm not stressed about holiday gift giving, I know many others are. I'd be interested in what you have to say.

People's emotions and feelings about the holidays are complicated and mixed. When asked how they feel about the holidays, one poll indicated that 80 percent of the respondents found them stressful, yet in another poll asking the same question, 70 percent said, "I love the holidays!" For most it is probably a combination where our fanciful selves (sleigh bells ringing, chestnuts roasting) love the holidays, whereas our practical selves (last-minute shopping, racing the kids from one relative to the next) can find them stressful. However, one statistic that is consistent is that 45 to 55 percent of people polled said they spend too much on gifts. Gift giving can stressful for a variety of reasons.

Hats off to you and your family for finding a way to reduce, if not totally eliminate, the stress that can result from a long list of gifts to be selected, purchased, wrapped, and delivered, not to mention the time and expense involved. It is worth looking at your point about others thinking the family grab bag is a great idea, but being reluctant to pursue it.

For many it is a matter of family traditions, and this can be a mixed bag. On the one hand, because they are established and practiced ways of doing things, traditions can be binding, predictable, and comfortable. In some families traditions are viewed as sacrosanct, so anyone who suggests changing them in any way, especially a newcomer to the family, can be really going out on a limb. Having a heart-to-heart talk with the older generations may be worthwhile, since they are typically the enforcers of the family traditions. If a grandparent decrees that the family gift-giving tradition is changing from one gift purchased for everyone to doing a grab bag, this can be a quick transition.

For many, explaining to the enforcers of the traditions the reasons for wanting to do a grab bag or some other variation on gift-giving traditions may be a simple solution, especially when highlighting the economic burden of buying everyone a present. Below are Six Guidelines for Giving and Receiving Gifts I wrote to help reduce some of the stress around gift giving and to give an impetus to consider changing burdensome gift-giving traditions.

Guidelines for Giving and Receiving Gifts

1. Help your child create a "gift wish list."

At a very young age, children learn to start a sentence with "I want . . . a new game, a certain toy, an electronic device." Keep a running list of all these I-want items for your child and if you hear your child request a certain toy more than once, add it to the gift wish list. She says, "I want . . . ," you say, "Fine. Let's add it to your gift wish list and then we can consider it as a birthday or holiday gift."

This approach honors your child's desire to want something without forcing you to take any immediate action. Then when appropriate gift-giving time is on the horizon, you can prioritize the wish list with your child—some items will drop off and others will be added. When grandparents and others ask what they can get for your child, you reference her gift wish list. In some instances, especially for older kids saving up for something more expensive, you can suggest that the gift giver contribute towards the purchase of the desired item.

In all cases, keeping a gift wish list for your child has several benefits: It helps him learn deferred gratification; it cuts down on disappointments; it eliminates the exchange frenzy; it helps gift givers feel confident that they're giving something that is truly of value or interest to a child.

2. Expand the wish list to include events and experiences.

Your child's gift givers typically think of purchasing something material, but including on the wish list events and experiences as gifts can be incredibly enriching and valuable. Suggest to grandparents that they plan a special day with your child for her birthday. Think how excited your child will be to learn that as a gift Grandma and Grandpa are taking her to the circus, or to the latest Disney movie followed by pancakes at the local diner, or for art lessons at the museum. The possibilities are endless.

Also, doing things together are gifts that can delight your child and create lasting and cherished memories, e.g., making Grandpa's special cookies with him, learning to knit with Grandma, scrapbooking with Aunt Linda, woodworking with Uncle Hank. In addition to these being gifts that your child will always remember with love and fondness, they are gifts that your budget-conscious gift givers can feel good about, both financially and emotionally.

3. Emphasize graciousness and gratitude when receiving gifts.

Children often need parental help in accepting gifts graciously. Prior to your son's opening his birthday or holiday presents, review with him the cardinal rule of accepting gifts: "Even if you are disappointed, always look at the gift giver and thank him for such a wonderful gift." Practice this with your child before the opening of gifts: "Let's be clear. What are you going to say and do after you open each gift?"

You can also help your child be a gracious gift receiver by handing him each gift to be opened, making sure he opens each card and either reads it himself or it is read to him. This cuts down on the out-of-control, crazed jumping from one gift to the next and not appropriately acknowledging the gift and the gift giver.

There may be times you will want to prepare your child in advance for a certain disappointment: "Your grandmother tried very hard to get you something in the color you would have preferred, but she wasn't able to, so you need to remember to be pleased when you open her gift, even though you may really be feeling disappointed."

Another way to teach graciousness and gratitude in receiving gifts is to space out when they are given. Of course you'll want your child's gift givers to enjoy watching the gift being opened in their presence whenever possible, but there may be times you can withhold some gifts for "a rainy day."

For example, if you bought your child several holiday presents, consider not giving them all out during the holidays, but rather, save some of them and present them during the following weeks: "Oh, what a yucky day this is. We cannot go to the park and play, but I have a surprise for you. Daddy and I put aside one of your holiday presents and today seems like the perfect time to give you a rainy-day present."

If you do this enough, instead of your child saying, "I'm bored," you may find him asking if you happen to have any rainy-day presents around. If you do, you may want to pull one out. Rainy-day presents can be an easy and creative way to deal with an overabundance of presents, as well as increasing gratitude for each gift received.

4. Emphasize the joy of giving gifts.

Although getting pleasure from giving to others comes easier to some children than to others, all kids can benefit from being provided opportunities to be the gift giver. For example, you remind your child that Daddy's birthday is coming up. Saying "What can we do to make it a special day for him?" is a very different question from "What can we buy him?" There is certainly nothing wrong with thinking about purchases for him, but brainstorming and planning special things to do for and with Daddy helps your child appreciate the joy that comes from giving and making someone happy.

Even if your child is too young to offer much in the way of ideas for making Daddy's birthday special, sharing your ideas can help build the right foundation. "We can make Daddy his favorite breakfast and serve it to him in bed, we can draw special birthday place mats for the table and make him the spaghetti dinner he loves, we can buy him that new golf club he's been eyeing and make our own wrapping paper for it, we can rent his favorite family video and watch it together while we eat popcorn," and the list goes on.

It is all about doing things that will bring joy to someone else, and the more your child is part of planning special things for someone else, the greater the chances are that she will want to repeat the fun and pleasure that comes from putting a smile on someone's face.

5. Make thank-you notes a natural and expected part of the process.

While gifts are being opened, make sure someone is keeping a list of who has given which gift, as this list will come in handy for writing thank-you notes. All gifts, be they purchases, events, or experiences, merit a thank-you note. If the gift giver can invest the time, emotional energy, and money, then your child can certainly find the time to show her gratitude in an appropriate way—with an old-fashioned, low-tech, hand-written thank-you note. It is also recommended that only a couple notes a day be written to make the task feel more doable, especially for younger children.

For the pre-literate child, I suggest the parent writes out the complete thank-you note and then, by way of signature, the child can trace his hand or do a finger paint print. For the child with some writing skills, the parent can write out the bulk of the note and the child can sign his name and affix some "xoxo's." Most older kids can write the whole note alone, but for younger ones just mastering writing and spelling, I suggest a parent sit beside their child to offer help with spacing and spelling. I think it's a good idea for the child to always use a pencil to write his notes to ease erasing inevitable errors and not having to start from scratch, a sure activity spoiler.

Picking out the thank-you note can be something your child can participate in, from selecting ready-made ones, to hand-making them, to computer-created ones. Personalizing the thank-you notes can be fun for your child if you provide some stickers, markers, construction paper, and glue. Remind your child that many of his thank-you notes are going to end up posted on a refrigerator, so he'll want to send something which he can feel proud to have on display.

6. Be a good role model for giving and receiving gifts.

This is probably the hardest guideline to apply. As any parent or educator knows, children are always influenced more by what adults actually say and do, rather than by what we espouse we should be doing. If you want to teach your child certain values and behaviors about giving and getting gifts, then you need to consistently model those values and behaviors yourself.

Being a good model means that as the predictably ugly tchotchke from your aunt arrives every December, all your child should see from you is your appreciation for receiving the gift.

If you want to emphasize that spending time together with your child is as valuable a gift as getting a Tiffany's gift certificate, then tell your child that going to the zoo and having lunch together is what you really want for your birthday or holiday gift.

And finally, make sure your child receives a thank-you note from you about the special time you had together at the zoo, the lovely lunch that followed, and that you look forward to your next outing together.

{Readers' Comments}
Guidelines for Giving and Receiving Gifts

One reader writes, *"I love your list and would add thinking of giving gifts to causes and charities, which add an important dimension to all aspects of giving and receiving gifts."* This is a great suggestion.

Another reader wrote, *"Gramma Karen, you should make sure all your readers know about your concept of 'I'm an only child.' It's such a great idea for a gift. We are going to use it with our four grandchildren."* This is by way of explanation: For grandparents who have more than one grandchild in the same family, the idea of "I'm an only child" is to plan something special to do with each grandchild, without his/her siblings. It can be a day together or a weekend away, just the grandparents and one grandchild. The other siblings stay with their parents or other grandparents. I know of one little boy, when asked where he got a new book, he replied, "Oh, I got that book from Grandma when I was an only child." The kids love it and will even ask when they next get to be "an only child."

A reader e-mailed to say that she saw a TV clip recommending cardboard boxes of all sizes to play in; it showed the kids enjoying this activity more than their other gifts. To extend the idea, it would be fun to make a project of decorating the boxes.

And finally, the gift of togetherness is suggested by a young mom: *"This year, in lieu of doing a grab bag for the eleven cousins, we are going to surprise the kids (ranging in age from 6 to 19) and have them all open the same thing at the same time—it will be a ticket to a show or sporting event of some kind that we are all going to attend together."* The reader later let me know that the event they picked was a Celtics-Nets game. A great time was had by all!

{ PART 4 }

Power and Control
Letting Go of the Need To Win

{Chapter 24}

My Mother Is Hurtful towards My Son

Dear Dr. Gramma Karen:

I am in desperate need of some sound advice as some issues between my 12-year-old son Davey and my mother have come up. Of my three children, she's always favored him, felt a bond with him. Here is some background: My mom's behavior has always been very on and off. In years past while growing up I would leave home to stay with friends quite frequently to avoid the physical and mental abuse from both my parents. I spent years in therapy to get over the anger and resentment of my family life.

Lately my mother has been saying some not-so-very nice things about Davey to me. She purchased him a cellphone and pays for the monthly bill. She gives him guilt trips for not calling her to see how she is, or as she puts it, "being there for her." She said she has no use for him; she said he is stupid for not calling her to tell her about his grades.

Recently at a hockey celebration for Davey's team, as I was standing in the middle of a very crowded hallway talking to my son and friends, my mom approached Davey and very angrily told him, "Enjoy your cellphone." She stormed off, turned around again, and wagging her finger in his face said, "You're dead to me." Davey was very upset and heartbroken about my mother's harsh words. He can't understand how his actions prompted such hurtful language. Even worse was that the other parents witnessed this scene, and her behavior was the talk of our team celebration that evening.

I do not want to have a rift in my family, but I also do not want my mother saying hurtful things to my children. I agree with my husband who has always been adamant that no matter how inappropriate any of our parents' actions may have been over the years, we are lucky to have grandparents in our kids' lives and that we should cherish them while they are still here.

I want this family drama to end once and for all. Most people do not begin to understand how I continue to have a relationship with my mother. Regardless, she is my mother and she also has her good moments. I have tolerated the dysfunction my mother causes for my whole life, but I will not let my children be victims of any of it.

I just pray that this situation will be able to be resolved. I have three incurable disorders and this stress just makes my health worse.

I understand why many of your friends question why you continue to want to have a relationship with you mother, but since you and your husband are in agreement that you want your parents to have a presence in your children's lives, I will give you my advice on how that might work.

First, I don't think your mother's treatment of Davey is the core issue; rather, I think it is an example of a larger and even more serious issue. When you were growing up, you were physically and emotionally abused by your parents. These same people are now your children's grandparents, so my first piece of advice is that you never, ever, under any circumstances, leave your children alone with either your mother or father. Never. They have an irrefutable history of being child abusers, and even though you say your mother has "her good moments," your mother is unpredictable and can flare out of control at any time, much to your children's detriment. You and your husband need to protect your children from this destructive behavior. Therefore, one of you must always be with your children when their grandparents are around. This means your parents never take any of your children out of your sight, not for shopping, not for a movie, not to a restaurant, and most definitely not for a sleepover.

This brings me to the second part of my advice. You and your husband need to take control of the relationships between your children and your parents. Right now your mother controls your family relationships: If she is nice, things run smoothly. When she erupts, this throws everyone into a state of fear and trepidation. Currently, your mother determines the ebb and flow of what is going on, how family members are feeling, and how they behave. As you have learned, trying to have a rational conversation with her about her behavior does not work.

Monitoring and controlling how your mother behaves in front of your children is going to be extremely challenging for you and your husband. Gaining the confidence and courage to tell her she must immediately stop certain behaviors, or leave, is going to be very difficult, and that is why I feel strongly you are going to need professional help to learn how to deal effectively with her.

You have personal and successful experience working with a therapist, and now you must find one to work with you and your family. Your therapist will teach you and your family:

- How to take control of the safety and well being of your

children when your parents are around.

- What to say and do when your parents are behaving in threatening, unkind, bullying, and other unacceptable ways.
- How not to be victimized by or in any way made to feel at fault for your parents' behavioral problems and issues.
- What to say to your children when they are trying to understand your parents' irrational and angry behavior.
- How to help your children understand that they are not responsible for their grandparents' behavior.

If you do these two things, that is, first, starting right now, commit to never leaving your children alone with either of your parents, and second, locate and begin working with a family therapist, I think you and your family have a chance at keeping your parents in your lives in ways that do not put you, your husband, and most important, any of your children at risk of being hurt and/ or abused in any way by them. I hope you will take my advice, as I feel strongly that if you choose instead to let the situation continue as is, you are putting the safety and well being of your children at grave risk.

Two Months Later:

Kathy Provides an Update on Grandmother's Hurtful Behavior towards Grandson

Dear Readers:

Many readers e-mailed me to say how concerned they were for Kathy, a distraught mom, who described her mother's angry, unpredictable, often bullying behavior towards Kathy's 12-year-old son Davey. Two months later Kathy provided an update by answering some questions I asked her.

When I asked Kathy what changes, if any, she and her husband decided to make regarding their relationship with her parents, she responded: *"My husband and I decided to pull back a little from how close we were [with my parents] and how much time we spent with them so these things don't happen [grandmother's unpredictable behavior towards Davey]. My mother feels too close with my son; she actually told me she feels like his second mother, so obviously some distance needed to be made in that regard . . . I discussed the situation with my mother about her behavior. However, she hasn't changed and went right back to how things were, badmouthing everyone in the family . . . We decided not to spend Easter with my family this year."* (In fact, Kathy did not have any contact with her mother for two months.)

How did you explain to your children any changes that you decided to make regarding your parents? *"I mostly talked to my son about the changes we were making. I let him know that I never want him in that position again where my mother can hurt him. I explained that if having a relationship with my mother made him uncomfortable after the way she hurt him, it was okay and he didn't have to forgive her until he was ready. I told him that I want him to be able to talk to me about how he feels about these things. My younger daughters were very upset about what their grandmother said to their brother, but I discussed with them how wrong their grandmother's behavior was and how sometimes adults say hurtful things. They are too young to understand fully, but my middle daughter was very standoffish with my mother the first time she saw her [after the incident] as she was very upset with her."*

What other changes have you made? *"I have not let my*

mother watch my children or be alone with them. She is very upset by this. She won't stop making comments about how it seems I don't want her around the kids, which is comical to me. For five months now she has not come to any of my children's activities—none of Davey's hockey playoffs, his state competition, the girls' soccer games, Davey's school chorus performance . . . nothing. Their other grandparents have been to all of the kids' activities. I asked my mother-in-law to watch the kids one weekend so my husband and I could have some time away. My mom is offended that I didn't ask her. The only time we have seen my parents since this all went down is when we went to their home. They have made no effort, yet my mom doesn't understand why I won't drop things when she wants me to come shopping with her."

Did you get any professional help or other advice? "I mentioned counseling to my mother. She laughed. She has always said, 'I don't have any problems, it is everyone else, so why should I go?' In the meantime, I have gone back to my counselor whom I haven't seen in years. He basically thinks my mother will never change, so it is my decision about whether I go forward with her in my life."

Where do things stand now? "The couple of months I did not talk to my mom were very peaceful and stress free. Having a relationship with my mom leaves me with hurt feelings about how she never does anything to help my family or be part of my children's lives, yet she is always doing things for my brother and his family. I question myself constantly on why I even deal with her, considering all she does is stress me out and upset me with her drama and complaining. I am tired of her making comments when I don't get to talk to her every day. My life is very busy with my three kids. My disorders have flared up from the stress as well. I just don't know why I put myself through this.

"I don't feel my mom will ever change. I am the only one who is capable of changing. I just don't know how much more I can put up with the same old thing from her, or if I can change enough to stop *letting her hurt me."*

Kathy, although you are still working through some issues about the future of your relationship with your mother, I hope you don't lose sight of the incredible courage you have shown in the past few months and the significant changes you've already made. You have:

- Taken control of your relationship with your mother by making it clear to her that you will not tolerate her unacceptable and hurtful behavior.
- Demonstrated to your children that you and your husband will always protect them from potential and actual harm from others, including their grandparents, by not leaving them alone with them.
- Come to accept that your mother is most likely not going to change, so it is up to you to make any changes.

Because you recently had time during which you had no contact with your mother, you can now assess the quality of life you and your family experience when your mother is involved and when she is not involved. This comparison, as well as the ongoing guidance of your counselor, will no doubt help you continue to make decisions that are in the best interests of you and your family.

I know my readers join me in thanking you for sharing your situation and for giving us an update. Your actions will inspire others who are dealing with challenging family relationships to do whatever needs to be done to protect their children from those who can cause them any emotional and/or physical harm.

{Chapter 25}

My Niece's Mother and Mother-in-Law Are Always Competing

Dear Dr. Gramma Karen:

My sister Dawn is the mother of Madge and grandmother of four-year-old Riley. I have a very close relationship with Dawn, whereas my relationship with my niece Madge is comfortable, but not one where I would feel comfortable giving her any parenting advice, especially since I am not a mother. Riley is an adorable and extremely bright little girl. Riley calls my sister Nonna; she calls her other grandmother Grandma.

What's bothering me involves Riley's two grandmothers, who seem to be competing with each other, trying to buy her love, bribing her with their one-upmanship. Here are some examples. Nonna will give Riley a book. Then when Grandma is visiting and hears about Nonna giving Riley a new book, Grandma immediately has a gift basket of books sent to Riley. Or, Grandma makes arrangements to take Riley on an all-day outing to the zoo. Nonna immediately plans a weekend trip for Riley. And so it goes.

My husband sees what's going on, too, but no one else in the family seems aware. Maybe it shouldn't bother me, but I don't think this competitive behavior between the grandmothers is good for Riley.

Do you have any thoughts?

The phenomenon you describe, competing grandparents, has been dubbed by one commentator as the Grandparent Olympics. "One cutthroat grandfather, who asked that his name not be used, calls it the 'grandparent wars—it's a game you play for keeps.' No one keeps statistics on grandparents gone wild. But Susan Stiffelman, a licensed marriage, child and family therapist, says she regularly sees a 'low-key desperation to be the most popular grandparent' " (http://www.boston.com/lifestyle/family/articles/2009/05/14/senior_games/).

In fact, Barbara Graham, a blogger and regular contributor to Grandparents.com suggests the competition between Riley's Nonna and Grandma is inevitable: "Love for our grandkids may unite us, but, like members of any pack, we sniff out the competition and jockey for position in the new order. Inevitably, the playing field is uneven. One set of grandparents may live close to the grandchildren and babysit regularly, another set may be able to afford lavish gifts and trips to Disney World, yet another grandparent may have the zip (and balance) to rollerblade alongside the kids. And so we worry and stew and compare ourselves to the competition."

I agree that the competition between grandparents may be an all-too-common occurrence in general, but I don't agree that it is inevitable. Yes, it is only natural that a grandparent wants to have a unique bond with a grandchild, but this desire for a special relationship becomes problematic only when a grandparent wants the grandchild to regard him/her as the Most Favored Grandparent. Hence the competition, a striving to outdo another grandparent, a desire to be acknowledged as better or more cherished. Although we can all agree that this type of competition for a child's love and affection is unhealthy and grounded in insecurity, it will continue until one of three things happens.

One simple and effective way to end the competition among grandparents is that the parents observe the jousting and dueling and they declare a cease and desist. They can do this by letting the grandparents know that they, the parents, need to be consulted before the grandparents give the grandchildren any gifts or plan any trips or experiences for them. Many young parents head off the potential for competition between the grandparents by making this a ground rule when the first grandchild is born. Because you have already said that you don't think your niece Madge would appreciate you initiating a discussion with her that involves her parenting, the option of suggesting she reign in the competing grandmothers with a cease and desist order probably is not a viable option for you.

A second option is to say nothing, and as Riley gets older, she herself may draw attention to the competing grandmothers. Their competing over her may make her uncomfortable and she may verbally express her uneasiness with their behavior: "I don't like it when you sort of fight over me." A worse situation would be if a grandchild discerns the grandmothers competing over him/her and the child becomes manipulative, for example, by making sure the purchases and events planned by one grandmother become known to the other with the intention of fanning the flames and upping the ante. A bit diabolical and extreme perhaps, but such manipulation could be an outcome in this type of situation, if it is left unchecked.

A third way for the competition to end is that one of the competitors, for example, your sister, drops out. No contenders, no competition. You said you have a close relationship with your sister, so it might make sense for you to approach her, perhaps along these lines: "Dawn, I have observed a family dynamic that involves you, Riley, and Riley's other grandmother. You need to know that my observation could hurt your feelings because it will require you to look at something I think you're doing. I worry about upsetting you, but because we all love and care about Riley, I want to share my observation with you, if you want me to do so."

You feel close with Dawn, so chances are she will be open to listening to you. You will want to share your observation objectively and non-judgmentally: "It seems that when either you or Grandma does something nice for Riley, the other grandmother immediately does something similar, but bigger or grander. To me, it looks and feels like a bit like a contest or a competition. I just wanted to share this observation with you." Wait for Dawn's response, and you'll then know how your sister feels about your observation.

Hopefully she will appreciate your good intentions and will give some consideration to what you've said. She may come to realize that she and Grandma both should want Riley to learn love is not a zero-sum game, meaning there is only so much love and as one gains love, another must lose some. On the contrary! One of the wonderful things about love is that there is no need to compete over it—it is self-generating and there can be more than enough for everyone.

If you decide to talk with your sister, you may help her focus on not being The Best Grandmother in Riley's estimation, but rather, to focus on just being the best grandmother she can possibly be. This also includes being as loving and supportive of the other grandmother as possible in a noncompetitive way. Game over.

{Chapter 26}

Condo Residents Make My Children Feel Unwelcome When We Visit Grandma

Dear Dr. Gramma Karen:

My mother lives in a gated condominium building in southern Florida. She loves it when my husband and I bring our three young children to visit. Her apartment is large enough that we can all comfortably live together. We've done this for years and we have always enjoyed these visits.

The problem is that some of the other residents make it very clear that they don't appreciate our children being around. They show their disapproval with stony looks and meant-to-be overheard comments, e.g., "Must be school vacation week. That takes care of our peace and quiet." The other visiting parents I see are always shooshing their kids as well. We stand guard and make sure our kids are whispering in the pool; they are scared to move, splash, or smile.

A couple of the residents have taken to complaining to the building management about our kids being loud and unruly in the pool (they're not!), and someone from the staff has come out to "discipline" them. My husband and I are thinking about staying somewhere else, such as a family-friendly hotel in the area, and having my mom come visit us. I know this would upset my mother as she loves having the kids around and fussing over them, but we're not sure what else to do.

According to the 2010 US Census, in the part of the state where your mom has her condo, the 65 and older population comprises 20 percent. This statistic can work to your advantage because it means there are lots of other grandparents around who share your mom's desire to have their grandchildren visit on a regular basis. These similarly-minded grandparents are your best allies in condo living, the ones you and your mom want to get to know. You can easily identify them because you see them with their grandchildren during most, if not all, holidays and school vacations. Make sure you and your mom chat with them, learn the names of their grandchildren, and arrange for your kids to play with them.

Then there are the grandparents whose children and grandchildren make rare appearances, if any at all. This may be due to a variety of reasons: The grandparents like their privacy and don't want the noise and inevitable disruptions to their schedules when the grandchildren stay with them; they feel they don't have room for them; geography and finances preclude visits; or sadly, these grandparents may have limited, strained, or nonexistent relationships with their grandchildren. The fact is that some grandparents and other seniors just don't like having children around. Alas, these are the ones who can make life unpleasant for you and your family when you're using common areas such as the pool, shuffle board, and game room. And sometimes it takes only one person to cause problems by constantly complaining.

My advice is to do a couple of proactive things. First, if

there is a group of people in the pool taking a water aerobics class or just "bobbing" together, you or your mom can approach them and let them know your kids would like to use the other end of the pool and you just want to make sure your children won't be bothering them. Typically, someone will say something like, "Oh, I have grandchildren! Don't worry about it. They'll be fine." Then every now and then, circle back to them to make sure your kids aren't disturbing them. This show of respect for them can go a long way, especially when one of the "grumpy ones," as I call them, begins to complain about your kids.

One or more of your allies may tell the grumpy ones that the kids are fine and to lighten up. And by the way, I think it is okay to tell your kids that certain people in the condo don't like kids and may even be rude to them. Ask your kids not to be rude to them, but urge them not to let the grumpy ones ruin things for them, either. Since your kids are young, you or your mother would always be around to run interference with the grumpy ones, if need be. At those times your kids are noisy or a bit unruly, as most kids are at one time or another, you make and/or have your kids make the appropriate apologies, even to the grumpy ones.

If it is someone on the staff who is admonishing your kids' behavior, you are perfectly justified in telling that person that he is to talk only to you if he has something to say about your kids' behavior: "We will take care of disciplining our children. Bring all your issues to us. Please do not discuss them with our children." A steely voice and cold stare are appropriate to reinforce your message of Stay Away from My Children/Grandchildren.

In defense of some condo dwellers who resent the young ones, in many cases they are perfectly justified. It is disruptive and annoying when kids are running around the lobby, pool, and other common areas yelling and being wild. When the parents and/or grandparents make obvious attempts to correct these behaviors, other people can sympathize as the caretakers try to do the right thing. However, when the caretakers don't try to curb the loud and unacceptable public behavior, they deserve the scorn of those around them.

I hope you will take my advice that you and your mom seek out other grandparents with visiting grandchildren. Stick together, form an alliance. Stay with your mom. Don't let the grumpy ones drive you out! Shoosh your kids when they need it, but don't shoosh them in anticipation of upsetting the grumpy ones, who are going to be upset by the kids' mere presence, anyway. As one condo building manager said when a grandmother asked him what to do about a grumpy one who was constantly complaining about her grandchildren, "Ignore her. Go and enjoy your family."

{Chapter 27}

I Don't Want My Stepmother's Dog Around My Children

Dear Dr. Gramma Karen:

My mom died a few years ago. Last year my dad married Dottie. My husband and I have a three-year-old daughter, Kelly. Here is the problem. Dolly has a rescue dog, Butch, and she insists he has to be with her all the time, and I mean all the time. Butch was at their wedding!

I don't trust Butch. I don't know his background, but he may have had some unfortunate history with kids because he growls at Kelly, who runs to us for protection. Dottie tells him to stop growling, and she tries to reassure us that Butch won't hurt Kelly. I've talked with my dad and Dottie, asking them to please keep Butch isolated in another room while we're at their house, but Dottie says that would not be fair to Butch because "this is his home and he's done nothing wrong." They won't visit in our home because I've told them they can't bring Butch. I talked privately with my dad but he says Butch is important to Dottie and he doesn't want to upset her. My husband and I are not sure what to do.

I daresay you and your husband know exactly what to do

and you've done it. One of your main parenting jobs is to keep your child safe, and if you feel apprehensive for any reason about Butch, then that really is the end of the discussion. You have clearly stated your boundaries: Under no circumstances is Butch to be free to approach Kelly. You've asked Dolly to restrain Butch and she has denied your request. (Alas, I suspect your recently-married dad fears being consigned to the proverbial marital dog house if he sides with you in any way.)

Dottie has a common response from many dog owners when their free-running canine charges up to someone: "Oh, he won't hurt you." Maybe yes, maybe no, but here are the facts (Centers for Disease Control and Prevention in Atlanta):

- There are approximately 4.7 million dog bite victims annually in the USA; this is 2 percent of the population. An American has a 1 in 50 chance of being bitten by a dog each year.
- There are about 800,000 dog bite victims annually requiring medical attention; 1,000 per day are treated in an emergency room (ER). This means one of every six dog bite victims ends up in the ER.
- In 2010 there were 34 fatal dog attacks in the USA.
- The odds that a bite victim will be a child are 3.2 to 1.
- Seventy-seven percent of injuries by dogs to children under 10 years old are facial.
- The majority of dog attacks (61 percent) happen at home or in a familiar place.
- The vast majority of biting dogs (79 percent) belong to the victim's family or a friend.

I don't know if you will find these facts reassuring ("only" 2 percent of people are dog bite victims each year), or they'll strike you as a reaffirmation of your fears, or you'll find them totally alarming and exceeding your worst fears. You and your husband can decide if you want to try again to share with your dad and Dottie the reasons why you are unwilling to take any chances with Butch having access to Kelly. It sounds like Dottie is stuck in "Love me, love-my-dog," and that can be a tough paradigm to shift. Perhaps you can convince your dad and Dottie that you want them to be part of your lives, especially for Kelly's sake, and how sorry you are that Butch cannot be a part of the family visits. Perhaps they will be willing to agree to some kind of compromise that could work for all of you. For example, one of them stays with Butch in another room while you visit with the other, or you invite them individually to your home to visit.

It would be sad indeed if Dottie and your dad decide that they are a threesome that must always include Butch, but if they take that position, at some point in her life Kelly is going to understand that her grandfather and step-grandmother decided that being separated from Butch to spend time with her was not a sacrifice they were willing to make. All you can do is keep extending the invitations, sans Butch, and hope they will respect your concerns.

In this situation, based on your distrust of a dog that already shows aggressive and unpredictable behavior by growling at your daughter, it is up to your dad and Dottie to accommodate you and your family, not the other way around.

{Chapter 28}

Mealtimes with My Sister's Kids Is a Nightmare

Dear Dr. Gramma Karen:

I am not a parent or a grandparent, but I am an aunt and I hope you'll address this issue. My sister Brenda and her husband Patrick have two kids, my niece Kathleen, age 5, and my nephew Frankie, age 3. I adore these kids and love being with them, except at mealtimes. I dread those!

Brenda and Patrick harangue the kids to eat with endless repetitions of "Eat this, eat that, one more bite, no treats until you eat this." The kids fuss, whine, and resist. It is so unpleasant I could just scream. I asked my sister if we could do something to make mealtimes for the kids more enjoyable, but she brushed me off and said they need to learn to eat right and to obey their parents. And to make it even worse, my parents (the kids' grandparents) do the exact same thing at mealtimes when they're babysitting. When I talked with them, they said they had to do what Brenda tells them to do.

I am single, have never been married and I don't claim to be any kind of an expert when it comes to raising children, but I can't believe mealtimes have to be so awful. I feel bad for the kids. Is there anything I can do?

Alas, your options are limited. I say this because the feeding of children seems to be an area where smart and normally rational parents become stuck in power and control dramas where the outcomes are consistently and predictably a lose-lose for both the parents and the children. Underpinning the eating battles is that many parents of young children, like Brenda and Patrick, mistakenly believe they can control all aspects of their children's eating.

Eating ends up a power play where the parents, again mistakenly, equate good parenting with their success in winning these unwinnable battles. The kids fight this control by outright refusing to eat, or by making the process difficult. If others are around, the young parents often get louder and more adamant that their kids follow their eating dictums, perhaps correctly suspecting they are being observed, and even worse, judged. It really is uncomfortable to witness.

As you point out, it is easy for Brenda and Patrick to dismiss your thoughts and input. You don't have any direct experience in raising children, you don't have a formal background in this area, and most important, Brenda and Patrick have not asked for your advice. In fact, they seem very committed to doing what they're doing. They've even trained the grandparents to carry the banner in their absence!

It sounds like Brenda and Patrick have a basic parenting philosophy, that is, a set of guiding principles about their kids' eating based on interspersing the use of controlling, coaxing, cajoling, begging, forcing, and making threats. This will continue unless they change their basic philosophy about what they want to be the goals and outcomes of their kids' feeding and eating habits. I have two excellent sources for you if you decide you want to approach Brenda and Patrick about reassessing their current philosophy, but for the reasons already discussed, your chances of influencing them are not good.

One is the philosophy developed and taught by eating specialist and author Ellyn Satter (http://www.ellynsatter.com/). She says, "Feeding demands a division of responsibility. Parents are responsible for the What, When, and Where of Feeding; Children are responsible for the How Much and Whether of Eating." In addition to her books, Ellyn's Web site is chock full of research and information to help parents (and aunts!) make this philosophy doable, ongoing and successful. I have to point out that her emphasis on the division of responsibility is difficult for many young parents to accept.

Another great resource is sociologist, researcher, teacher and Mommybites.com guest speaker, Dr. Dina Rose (to listen to her one-hour presentation, http://www.babybites.com/09/29/you-don%E2%80%99t-have-to-live-with-a-picky-eater-anymore-seminar-recap/; to visit her Web site It's Not About Nutrition, http://itsnotaboutnutrition.squarespace.com/).

I asked Dr. Rose to summarize her philosophy about children and eating for my readers. "My philosophy is simple: Eating right isn't about food, it's about behavior—what, where, why, when, and how much someone chooses to eat . . . if you want to teach children to eat right you have to focus less on the food and more on shaping their behavior . . . Unfortunately, our current culture of nutrition has created an environment where parents approach feeding their children with a nutrition-at-all-cost mentality. . . The goal of getting nutrients into kids, however, leads parents to . . . shape their kids' taste buds in the wrong direction (towards sweets and treats and away from fruits and vegetables) . . . and use of questionable feeding strategies, such as two more bites, trading peas for pie, etc., that backfire."

She goes on to say: "The solution is for parents to focus less on the food and more on shaping their children's habits... When parents focus on shaping habits, good nutrition always follows. Alternatively, when parents focus on nutrition, they often inadvertently end up teaching bad habits. It's one of the greatest paradoxes of parenting!"

You might start a conversation with Brenda and Patrick and your parents by saying you looked into what a couple of experts had to say about children and eating, you found what they have to say really interesting, and you want to share what you have learned with them. It is a long shot, but maybe one of them will be frustrated enough with the current eating routines to want to learn about something different.

{Chapter 29}

My Niece and Nephew Are Spoiled Rotten

Dear Dr. Gramma Karen:

I'd like your advice on what to do about my nine-year-old niece, Abigail, and my eleven-year-old nephew, Parker. They are two of the most spoiled, ill-mannered, and unpleasant children you'll ever see. They constantly complain about being bored, even though they are allowed to buy whatever they want whenever they want. Their father (my brother), a successful businessman, travels a lot and doesn't spend much time with them. Their mother (my sister-in-law, SIL) makes excuses for their rude behavior: "They're just kids being kids. They'll outgrow it."

It is embarrassing when Abigail and Parker bark orders at the staff in their building ("Get our packages") or are uncivil to serving staff ("Gimme a hamburger with fries") or worse yet, telling their mother at the dinner table they'd rather Facebook their friends then talk with her about their day at school. My SIL just takes it. On the rare occasion I've suggested the kids are being rude, she reminds me I don't have kids so I don't really understand.

I find myself trying to spend as little time as possible with Abigail and Parker, but once every couple of months, I take care of them for the weekend so my SIL and brother can go away alone. I started doing this when they were young, and in the beginning I really enjoyed my time with them, as they were sweet and lovable. Now when they stay with me they don't pick up after themselves, they leave wet towels on the floor, and they are discourteous to the staff in my building. Any advice?

Abigail and Parker seem to fit the "the spoiled child syndrome," first described by pediatrician Dr. Bruce J. McIntosh in his article published by the American Academy of Pediatrics in 1989. Dr. McIntosh writes: "The spoiled child syndrome is characterized by excessive self-centered and immature behavior, resulting from the failure of parents to enforce consistent, age-appropriate limits." Spoiled kids lack discipline, are manipulative, and are generally difficult to be around.

Many child development experts estimate that about five percent of kids are spoiled, but other researchers feel that this estimate is too low. For example, child psychologist Dr. Dan Kindlon, author of *Too Much of a Good Thing*, interviewed more than 1,000 parents, and roughly 650 teenagers, and found that 60 percent of parents thought their kids were spoiled, and 15 percent of teens thought they, themselves, fit the definition.

Experts agree that children become spoiled and feel entitled when they are overindulged by their parents. Psychologist Phillip Calvin McGraw, best known as Dr. Phil, goes so far as to say that parental overindulgence "is one of the most insidious forms of child abuse." He elaborates on what he means by this and offers advice on what parents can do about overindulged children (http://www. drphil.com/articles/article/94).

When parents spoil their kids, it is up to these same parents to unspoil them, but this can happen only when a parent recognizes that he/she has spoiled children and wants to do something about it. When you are with your SIL and/or your brother, as the parents, they are in charge of Abigail and Parker. So, as an aunt who has not been asked to get involved in the much-needed "unspoiling," your best and strongest course of action is to use your home team advantage.

In team sports, the term home team advantage describes the advantage—usually a psychological advantage—that the home team (that would be you) is said to have over the visiting team (Abigail and Parker when they stay with you) as a result of playing in familiar facilities (your apartment) and in front of supportive fans (your building staff). Under these circumstances your brother and SIL have designated you *in loco parentis*, Latin for "in the place of a parent," which refers to the legal responsibility entrusted to you to take on some of the functions and responsibilities of a parent. My advice is: Go for it!

Next time your brother and SIL ask you to take care of Abigail and Parker in their absence, that is your opportunity to sit everyone down and let them know that you want to go over some ground rules before you agree to take care of the kids—ground rules to which your brother, SIL, and the kids must commit or they will need to make other caretaker arrangements.

Without sermonizing or mentioning past unacceptable or rude behavior, you clearly state what is important to you in terms of Abigail and Parker's behavior when you're in charge.

Here's your chance to set expectations and boundaries. Have just a few and be specific. For example, you might say, "Good manners at all times are important to me. I need you to say please and thank you to the staff in my building and to servers in restaurants, as well as to me. I need you to be responsible for some chores, including, picking up all your towels, clothes, toys, and games from the floor when you're done with them, and putting your dishes in the dishwasher after meals. And finally, no electronics may be used at the dinner table." To drive the point home, you can write these out as a contract of commitment and have your niece and nephew sign it.

I think you get the idea. You make it clear that the discussion is not a negotiation, but rather, a setting out of your ground rules. They either commit to them, or they don't. If your ground rules are unacceptable to your brother, SIL, and/or the kids, you calmly and unemotionally say that you won't be able to take care of Abigail and Parker. If an agreement is reached but the kids hassle you when you're taking care of them, you can call your brother and SIL and ask them to come get Abigail and Parker immediately, as commitments have not been kept.

Granted, the tough love I'm recommending may not win you any popularity contests, but most important, you may help Abigail and Parker learn some discipline and manners, at least while they're in your presence. It's a start.

Chapter 30

My Grandson's Mother Is Keeping Him From Me

Dear Dr. Gramma Karen:

When I lost my son in a car accident two and a half years ago, his son Randy was three at the time. Even though my son and my grandson's mother never married, she was very generous and let my second husband and me spend a lot of time with our grandson for the first ten months after the accident. In fact, for several months, Randy spent entire weekends with us while his mother worked part time or had some time alone with friends. We never minded, as it gave us some extra time with our grandson.

When Randy started school, everything changed. His mother had a new boyfriend, and Randy had some behavioral problems at school. He apparently threw a book in class and when scolded, he said, "My grandmother lets me throw books," which, of course, I would never let him do. I tried talking to his mom, offered counseling, but nothing would work. She basically shut us out except for an occasional hour visit with her present. Every time I would ask to see him, she always "had plans."

I then took her to court for visitation. I was given a weekend visit every other month, a once-a-week phone call and a week during the summer. (I had asked for a weekend every month, but she abruptly moved away from the area. The judge thought it would be difficult for Randy to have to travel so much.)

Here is my problem. My husband (whom Randy calls Granddad) and I have talked with him every weekend as agreed. However, his mother has now decided she no longer wants Randy and Granddad to talk with each other since my husband has no "blood" connection to Randy. Now our grandson says, "I don't want to talk to Granddad," and we suspect she is telling him to say that. When I asked Randy why, he said, "I just don't want to."

My husband is the most kind, loving man alive, and he is so crushed. On top of this, Randy's mother is now monitoring what our grandson says to us. No matter how much I try to bring Randy into the conversation, it is usually a yes or no answer. Our talks used to last at least ten minutes, now I'm lucky if I can get him to talk for more than five. I have tried carrying the conversation by talking about things around the house or some of his neighborhood friends, without success. I am so very worried that she will ruin our relationship. Can you help, please?

Your situation is sad and heart wrenching in many ways, beginning with the sudden and tragic loss of your son. Then as you are enjoying a relationship with your grandson, to have your grandson's mother inexplicably begin to limit your access to him is unimaginably painful.

You asked for advice on how to maintain a relationship with your grandson. Let's start by acknowledging what your experience with the legal system has probably confirmed: Yes, grandparents in the U.S. do have some rights and can seek visitation with grandchildren, but those rights tend to be limited and vary from state to state. In fact, in some states, unless grandparents have been named legal guardians, their visitation rights can be nonexistent. Other states have statutes based on what is best for the child regarding visitation with grandparents, while other state statutes grant visitation only if the grandparents can verify they have had custodial care at some point in the child's life.

To understand the complexities of how grandparents' visitation varies from state to state, I recommend reading "Do Grandparents Have the Rights They Should?" (http://www. grandparents.com/gp/content/expert-advice/legal/article/ dograndparentshavetherightstheyshould.html#ixzz20W07gin7).

For a summary of each state's statutes regarding grandparents' visitation, these two sites are helpful: (1)http://grandparents.about.com/od/grandparentsrights/a/ VisitationRightsByState.htm; (2) http://family.findlaw.com/child-custody/summaries-of-state-law-grandparent-visitation-and-custody.html.

Alas, the statutes in your specific state are intertwined with custody (not your issue) and are not straightforward. Hence, your grandson's mother is currently in the driver's seat regarding your visitation with Randy. One suggestion I have is that your talk with other lawyers in your area who specialize in family matters and grandparent visitations, many of whom offer a free consultation, just to explore the possibility that different legal tactics may gain you a different outcome than the limited one under which your visitation is currently defined (http://law.findlaw.com/).

Meanwhile, while you explore legal expertise, your

immediate goal is to maintain a connection with Randy. Because it is impossible to discern Randy's mother's reasons for wanting to limit or eliminate your access to Randy, you must do whatever you can to help her see you as nonthreatening to her as a parent and to Randy as a grandparent. This means not questioning or in any way being defensive or antagonistic with her, but rather, being totally accommodating. As she throws up barriers and obstacles to your spending time with Randy, and as unfair and difficult as this may be to do, I urge you to acquiesce to her demands, within reason, of course.

Accommodating her may cause you great inconvenience and financial sacrifices, but I suggest you do whatever she asks of you to ensure she cannot describe you to the courts as unfriendly, uncooperative, or a poor role model. Regrettably, Granddad's desire to be part of Randy's life should probably go on hold right now. Randy's mother's statement about there being no blood connection is correct and Granddad has no legal basis whatsoever to be part of Randy's life.

As strained as your interactions are with Randy right now, your unwavering love and devotion to him may be the foundation on which your future relationship with him builds. As he gets older, he may ask that you (and Granddad) be more involved in his life, and his mother may be comfortable enough with you to honor his request.

PART 5

Values, Beliefs, and Principles
The Need to Consider Accommodation

{Chapter 31}

I Don't Want to Vacation with My Unpleasant Brother-in-Law

Dear Dr. Gramma Karen:

My sister Debbie is married to Brad, who is a jerk. Brad speaks disrespectfully to my sister and seems to care only about his motorcycle. When he is around us he is rude, sulky, and self-centered, barely answering us when we try to converse. He drifts from job to job and yet expects Debbie, who is a full-time teacher, to do all the housework and take care of their two kids, a five year-old girl and a three-year-old boy. Both are really nice kids. My husband and I also have two children, a six-year-old girl and a four-year-old boy.

Here's where you can help us. My wonderful parents, with whom we are very close, want to take all of us on a week-long cruise; they are paying for everything. We love the idea of the four cousins having this special time together and our being with Debbie and my parents, but we cannot imagine spending a week with Brad. How do we decline without hurting my parents' feelings?

You don't.

At the risk of hurting your feelings I want to suggest you

stop focusing on Brad—making the cruise about how miserable Brad will make you—and focus instead on what you can do to make this the best possible experience for your parents, Debbie, and the four cousins. I suspect your parents know Brad is a jerk and are probably worried about Debbie and her marriage and how everything might be affecting her children. Your parents want to do something unique and memorable. This is the critical question you have to answer: Do you and your husband have it in you to join your parents in trying to do something nice for the family?

I suspect your parents probably put a lot of time and thought into planning something that would make it easier for you to accept their invitation. They didn't rent a vacation home where you'd be in close contact with Brad. Rather, they chose a cruise. A cruise means you'll have your own stateroom and privacy and you all get a break from the usual household chores. A cruise also means there are lots of daily activities going on so you'll all probably be doing different things during the day, taking turns being with the children, and covering each other to pursue your own activities. Your parents may expect everyone to have dinner together, and if Brad joins you, you may find his presence a nonissue as everyone is happily chatting about their day and what they did and making plans for the following day.

Whatever decisions and choices Debbie may make in the future, it is important that she feels your love and support. If you do not go on the cruise, Debbie will most likely know it is because you don't want to be around Brad. But in rejecting Brad, you are also rejecting your parents, Debbie, and her children. So here is another question for you to answer: How important is it to you to make an obvious statement about Brad when the rest of your family, people you really care about, are penalized as a result?

I know you were looking for help to decline your parents'

invitation, and instead I gave you advice about why you should accept their invitation. You described your parents as "wonderful." This probably means they have been there for you every step of the way as you were growing up and that they continue to make themselves available to you and your children.

Look at this as payback for all the wonderful things your parents have done for you through the years. Accepting your parents' invitation for a family cruise is your opportunity to show your gratitude in a way that will mean so very much to them. Make this about you coming through for your parents and you might find the idea of this family cruise a really fun and special thing to do.

{Chapter 32}

My Grandson's Mother Is a Poor Role Model

Dear Dr. Gramma Karen:

    My grandson Robb is five. My son Ed and Robb's mother Barbara never married. Ed has a history of addiction problems and claims he can't take care of Robb full time, so Robb lives with Barbara during the week and with Ed and me on weekends in my house. I lost my husband a few years ago and need to work full time for several more years.

    I worry about Robb for a lot of reasons, but my main concern is that Barbara has one guy after the other living with her. Legally there is nothing Ed can do about that because they were never married and there are no custody papers. Robb talks with me about "mommy's new friends," so I know what's going on. Barbara's mother (Robb's other grandmother) seems like a very nice woman, but she isn't very involved in Robb's life. Even though she has tried, she has not had any success in getting Barbara to change her ways.

    I am very bothered by Barbara living with one guy after the other. What kind of message does this send to Robb? What does it say about relationships? What can I do?

Before we talk about your particular situation, I must say that as a grandparent helping raise your grandson, you are one of America's unsung heroes. And you are not alone. According to the U.S. 2010 Census, almost 7.8 million children live in homes where grandparents or other relatives are the householders. Over 5.8 million children live in grandparents' homes and nearly 2 million children live in other relatives' homes. More than 2.5 million grandparents are taking on the direct responsibility for raising their grandchildren.

Although most caretaker grandparents express hope as they try to do right by their grandchildren, they also report many anxious feelings and emotions, including: a sense of failure in raising their own children; a fear that they will prove to be failures in raising their grandchildren; resentment towards their children who have foiled their retirement plans; guilty for feeling resentment towards their children and/or grandchildren.

Because over 60 percent of grandparents raising their grandchildren are still in the work force, they also report feeling exhausted and often isolated. While many friends in their age bracket are talking about retirement and planning trips, caretaker grandparents are worrying about week-to-week paychecks, their grandchildren's everyday requirements, and their futures. And yet, even though this is not what they want to be doing, caretaker grandparents put their own aspirations on hold and do whatever they can to take good care of their grandchildren. Unsung heroes, indeed.

With regard to your situation, you are correct in describing Barbara as a poor role model to help Robb learn how to establish and maintain healthy and fulfilling relationships. Sadly, the reality is that Barbara will most likely continue her search for love and happiness via her revolving door of live-in relationships. Your chances of getting Barbara to change her behavior are slim, so I suggest you not put your time, effort, and energy into trying to change her, but rather, continue doing what you're doing: Stay the course and be Robb's anchor, his rock. Maybe he can't count on his mother or father to model solid and life-affirming values, but he can count on you. Many grandchildren who grew up under less-than-desirable circumstances have become happy and contributing adults, and many attribute the positives in their lives to their grandparents: "If it weren't for my grandparents, I never would have been able to . . ."

Robb may already suspect that there is something a bit off about "mommy's new friends." The challenge for you is to keep it comfortable for Robb to share with you what's going on when he's living with his mother, and resist the understandable urge to criticize her in any way because you risk his clamming up. Kids are typically very astute at seeing their loved ones' shortcomings and inadequacies, especially as they get older and have more bases of comparison, but Barbara is and always will be his mother. You can help Robb honor that unalterable fact by consistently living your values to counteract her destructive ones.

If Robb asks you why Mommy does such and such, you can ask him what he would prefer her to do instead. In this way, you can help him see alternatives, some of which he might even discuss with his mother.

You can also say something along these lines: "We are all looking for love and happiness, your mother included. Some things we do work better than others in this search. The important question for you is what are you going to do to find love and happiness in your life? And I want you to know that I will help you." This kind of message can empower Robb and give him hope that regardless of unfortunate behaviors and outcomes in the lives of others, e.g., his parents, he can make decisions that will help, rather than hinder him. He will also know that he can count on his grandmother every step of the way.

I have another consideration for you: While you're busy taking care of Robb, I urge you to take care of yourself, too. You might, for example, find it reassuring to meet with others who are dealing with similar concerns by joining a support group comprising caretaker grandparents. To locate support groups in your area, you may want to contact the National Committee of Grandparents for Children's Rights, a nationwide network of grandparents, community members, and professionals (http://www.grandparentsforchildren.org/chapters.asp).

Here is my closing thought: When we see men and women in uniform on the street or in airports or on the subway, many of us thank them for their service. I think you and all caretaker grandparents also merit a similar nod of gratitude. Thank you!

{Chapter 33}

My Friend's Granddaughter's Style of Dress Is Embarrassing

Dear Dr. Gramma Karen:

My friend Aileen, a grandmother of 73, does not know what to do, if anything, about this situation. Her granddaughter, Madison, a sophomore in high school, is doing well, both academically and athletically. She also has wonderful social skills with her peers and older adults. However, she has shown up at recent family gatherings and holidays in scanty attire that Aileen finds most inappropriate and offensive. Aileen's husband, Madison's grandfather, is also embarrassed.

The grandparents have a very good relationship with their daughter and her husband, and also with Madison. They've tried to nicely express their concerns to the mom, dad, and granddaughter. The granddaughter just attributes her grandparents' comments about the way she dresses to their being old and out of touch. The parents just shrug their shoulders.

I didn't think too much about this conversation with Aileen, thinking, well, how bad could it be? Then recently, I ran into Madison as she was heading into school, and I was, to say the least, shocked and appalled at what she had on, or didn't have on. I can only assume there is no school dress policy, and apparently there is a lack of good judgment on the part of the granddaughter and the parents. What is some good advice?

There are two main issues embedded in this situation. First there is the issue of the grandparents, who, when they try "to nicely express their concerns," are greeted with rejection by their daughter and granddaughter. Madison, who sounds like a wonderful young woman in so many important ways, may not realize and/or doesn't care that she's being disrespectful to her grandparents. Alas, by shrugging off the grandparents' concerns, Madison's parents are reinforcing and validating the disrespect. (It is not known if the parents' shrugging off how Madison dresses means they don't have an issue with her choices, or if they've lost control of the situation and are resigned.)

It would be an unreasonable request if the grandparents were asking Madison to change totally her style of dress under all circumstances, at all times. They're not. They are asking that she dress more conservatively when she is spending time with them. It is a simple, straightforward matter of Madison deciding what is more important to her, respecting her grandparents' request that affects her on rare occasions, or her being adamant about dressing how she wants to dress, no matter what.

Being nice about it did not work for the grandparents, so they may want to consider a stronger, more explicit message. "Madison, when you're with us, we would so appreciate it if you didn't wear sausage-tight clothes and expose your gluteal cleft, breasts and cleavage, navel and upper thighs. It makes us uncomfortable as we feel we're seeing waaaaaaay too much of you." Hearing her grandparents use this terminology may embarrass Madison into wearing less revealing clothes when she is with them, but Madison may again ignore their request.

The second issue you raise, how Madison dresses for school, is about school dress codes and uniforms. Madison's school probably has a dress code. The National Center for Education Statistics (http://nces.ed.gov/) estimates that over 70 percent of public schools do have one. Although dress codes are always being legally challenged as limiting freedom of expression, these challenges typically are superseded by the need to provide a safe environment—that is, "Most measures in school dress codes are intended to limit exacerbating messages and provocative displays, whether intentional or unintentional."

Whether dress codes are enforced by school personnel is a different issue, but regardless of the extent to which the schools are enforcing them, parents should nevertheless fully enforce them. Teaching their kids decorum, common sense, and how to dress and behave appropriately, based on circumstances, is a basic parental responsibility. For those schools lacking a dress code, parents can push for one either directly with their school administration or through their local Parent Teacher Associations (PTAs).

School uniforms have been a mainstay of most private schools, and even though there is much controversy, more public schools have been requiring them. In fact, the U.S. Department of Education published that in 2009–10, about 23 percent of public school principals reported that their school required students to wear uniforms, an increase from 12 percent in 1999–2000. Other relevant statistics include: Average annual cost to parents for school uniforms is $249; 95 percent of teachers feel wearing school uniforms has resulted in positive student behavior (only 37 percent of parents agree) http://www.statisticbrain.com/school-uniform-statistics/.

Other research that supports school uniforms in the public schools revealed that 68 percent of the parents believed the uniform policy improved overall academic performance. Eighty-eight percent of the parents thought the code reduced teasing between boys and girls. Eighty-four percent felt the uniform code promoted equality between the sexes. Perhaps most revealing was the fact that 80 percent of the girls and 62 percent of the boys reported liking to wear uniforms (http://news.fresno.edu/11/11/2007/pros-and-cons-school-dress-code).

So, where does all this leave Aileen, a grandmother who finds her granddaughter's mode of dress embarrassing? As already suggested, she and her husband might deliver to Madison and her parents a more strongly worded request that Madison accommodate them by dressing more conservatively when they are together. If Madison refuses, they can either accept her decision, or, depending on the extent of their discomfort, they can either limit or eliminate time spent with her. I am hopeful that if Madison doesn't come through for them on her own, then her parents weigh in on the side of expecting her to show some respect for the grandparents.

My grander hope is that all parents help their children learn about fashion expectations and appropriateness so that school administrators, teachers, and employers don't have to do it in their stead.

Here is an update: Madison's grandfather asked her to dress more conservatively in the future when she was with her grandmother and him as a sign of her love and respect for them. Madison agreed to do so. End of issue.

{Chapter 34}

I Don't Want to Be Called Grandma

Dear Dr. Gramma Karen:

I have no children from my first marriage, but my second husband has two grown children from his first marriage. They are nice kids and I get along just fine with both of them.

My stepdaughter is expecting her first child in a few months, and she is very excited, as are we all. My problem is that she has said she wants the baby to call me Grandma. The truth of the matter is that I don't want to be called Grandma. I am several years younger than my husband and I don't think of myself as a grandmother. I want the baby to just call me by my first name, Charlotte (fictitious first name), but everyone in the family is putting pressure on me to be called Grandma.

I'm interested in how you would help me convince them that it's okay for the new baby to call me by my first name.

It can be difficult to switch roles from parent to grandparent, and in your case from stepmother to step-grandmother. The reality is that if a grandparent wants to be a persona grata, he/she has to make concessions and be willing to acquiesce and accommodate a lot, always mindful that he/she is not in the driver's seat anymore: Their kids and their kids' spouses are when it comes to parenting the grandchildren.

However, when it comes to what the grandparent is called by the grandchildren, this is one area where the grandparent may want to compromise, but he/she definitely should not accept a name that is not comfortable. It is wonderful that your stepfamily wants to confer true grandmother status on you by calling you Grandma, but that's not going to work for you. You may find family members want you to explain why you don't want to be called Grandma, but you don't have to explain yourself in any detail, unless you want to. You can simply say you'd rather be called something else.

You stated a preference that the grandchildren simply call you by your first name, and this is an option, but I can see where this might seem a bit aloof and impersonal by other family members, even in this day and age of great informality, as it in no way calls out any specialness in your relationship with your step-grandchild. Some families use traditional nomenclature for grandmother in foreign languages, often based on ethnic backgrounds, e.g., "Oma" (Dutch, German), "Yia-Yia" (Greek), "Nonna" (Italian), "Abuela" (Spanish), "Bubbe" (Yiddish). For an extensive list of What People Around the World Call Their Grandparents, see http://www.namenerds.com/uucn/grannyworld.html. This may give you some ideas.

Sometimes the kids themselves come up with a name, either deliberately or through mispronunciation. For example, there is Aunt Janet, who was called Nana (Nah-nah) by the first-born grandson in the family who couldn't say Janet. That was 50 years ago, and Janet is still called Nana by everyone in this large family. Another example is the grandmother who decided she wanted to be called Mim, based on a dream shared with her by her best friend. Her husband decided he wanted his grandsons to call him GP for Grand Poppa.

In my family I elected to be called Gramma Karen because I felt it only right that my son-in-law's mother be Grandma because her daughter had the first grandchild and she wanted to be Grandma. Her husband went with Papa, and my husband chose to be called Peps.

Then there is my grandson Nicholas who calls me Mimi, even though all the many children in my life, biological and non-biological, call me Gramma Karen. He knows I am Gramma Karen, but he calls me Mimi. Fine by me.

And that really is the point: Whatever you decide to be called, it does need to be fine by you, and being called Grandma is not. With a little creativity perhaps you can find a comfortable moniker that acknowledges both the uniqueness of your status as a step-grandparent and the desire of your family for you to be included in a special way.

{Chapter 35}

I Worry My Grandchildren's Wealthy Parents Will Spoil Them

Dear Dr. Gramma Karen,

My husband and I will soon be first-time grandparents when our daughter delivers twins. We are over-the-moon happy, but we do have a major worry. Both our daughter and her husband are successful bankers. They make a lot of money and the way they live their lives is very different from ours. They have a full-time staff of a driver, a housekeeper, and they each have a personal assistant; they plan on hiring two nannies, one for each baby.

We feel the way our daughter and son-in-law live is excessive and just not normal. We get so embarrassed when they send their driver to pick us up at our modest apartment in Queens, where we raised our daughter. We worry that our grandchildren are doomed to being spoiled children who go through life feeling superior, entitled, and expecting everything to be handed to them. Are we worried over nothing? Should we say anything to our daughter and son-in-law?

Parents typically say they hope their children will be better off than they are. It sounds like your daughter and your son-in-law are successful beyond the highest hopes you may have had for them. Compared to your financial circumstances their lifestyle may seem "excessive and not normal," but a more accurate way to describe their situation is to say it is rare (a group comprising 40,000 to 3 million Americans, depending on how you define what it means to be affluent, rich and super rich).

You and your husband need to accept that their lifestyle is now commonplace for them. When they send a chauffeured car to drive pick you up, they are not doing it to embarrass or impress you, but rather, because this is their usual transportation. When you're about to go somewhere, you think about subway schedules—and that's your "normal." Your daughter and son-in-law have a different normal—they're thinking about how long it is going to take their driver to get to them. No rights, no wrongs, just a different frame of reference.

Saying "Thank you" is all that is needed when they do nice things for you. When you want to reciprocate their kindness and generosity, you can do so in ways that are fun, special, and within your budget, e.g., making them their favorite dinners, putting together a photograph album from an event you did together, hosting them for the theater, or a trip to a museum. Focus on spending time together. This is something you can also make central in your relationships with your grandchildren, too. In short, I am suggesting you accept (and enjoy!) your daughter and son-in-law's lifestyle decisions and be gracious when they share their good fortune with you. If you want to say anything, tell them how proud you are of them and how much you appreciate all the nice things they do for you.

However, your concerns are warranted when you ask if there are any potential downsides to being a privileged child. For example, author and clinical psychologist Madeline Levine, Ph.D., researched the following question: Which group of children do you think will fare their teen years more easily? Children of parents who are financially succssful, or children of parents who are struggling financially?

Surprisingly and paradoxically, research conducted by Dr. Levine and other experts establishes that children from wealthy and affluent homes are at significantly greater risk of developing serious emotional problems precisely because of their privileged circumstances. That is, teens from affluent, well-educated families are less happy, less confident, and prone to higher rates of depression and suicide attempts than are their less affluent counterparts.

This finding may seem counterintuitive. It would seem that if children are readily given what they want, they will be happy, satisfied, well-adjusted, and have strong self-esteem as they head into and through their teen years. However, this is not always the case. The research indicates that the children of the wealthy and affluent are experiencing disproportionately high levels of emotional problems.

Dr. Levine explains: "Because money and material objects are plentiful in comfortable homes, they often become the default motivator when parents want to change their children's behavior." When parents use potential purchases to try to change their kids' behavior, the results are often disappointing. In fact, many times when a parent promises to buy something the child wants if they behave, or if they do their homework, this may really mean the parent is frustrated and perhaps feeling all options have been exhausted, leading to a fallback position: When all else fails, pull out the credit card and head for the mall or do some online shopping.

Other related points include the fact that shopping can give kids a false sense of security and control over their lives. A new purchase can create a momentary good feeling, but it is actually not a sustainable way to reduce stress. As soon as the thrill of the purchase wears off, the troublesome feelings of insecurity or inadequacy resurface, only to be replaced by yet other yearnings for purchases to keep them at bay. And so the unfulfilling cycle of consumerism continues, over and over.

Many parents funding this unfulfilling cycle of consumerism are confused. On the one hand, it makes sense at some level that parents would unconditionally share their good fortune with their children. What good does it do to have money if it isn't used to bring pleasure and delight, especially for one's children? On the other hand, many parents find that somehow they never seem to be able to give their children enough. The kids keep asking for and getting more and more, and yet their behavior becomes even more challenging, and in many cases, outright bratty, with an increase in sullen demands. Somehow, in many affluent and wealthy households, the generous use of the credit card, which is supposed to be a problem solver, can be, in fact, a problem creator.

So what might affluent and wealthy parents do to address this issue? I suggest the simplest way is through the use of one word: budget. When it is consistently explained that budgeting requires planning and saving, a comment such as the following can become expected and accepted: "We did not budget for the new toy you would like, so we need to talk about it and plan ahead for it." This kind of conversation helps children of all ages deal with disappointment, learn to defer gratification, and most important, it decreases the chances of children developing attitudes of feeling entitled.

Less affluent parents talk about budgets out of financial necessity. Affluent and wealthy parents need to talk about budgets with their children out of developmental and emotional necessity, even though money is an abundant resource for them. Children from affluent homes need to appreciate that their fortunate circumstances are attributable to their parents, and that their main job in growing up is to acquire the education and tools to make their own way as adults. This basic understanding is critical in helping reduce the risk many affluent teenagers face by virtue of being raised in financially secure homes.

Depending on your comfort level, you and your husband might decide to discuss with your daughter and son-in-law the research discussed above. They may have their own concerns about the impact of wealth on their parenting and be open to you sharing with them what you have learned. At the very least you can make discussions about planning, budgeting, and saving a natural part of your relationship with your grandchildren.

{Chapter 36}

We Don't Want Any Hurt Feelings When We Pick Legal Guardians

Dear Dr. Gramma Karen:

My husband and I are working on our wills and we have some questions for you. Do you have suggestions about discussing guardianship issues with grandparents, just in case something should happen to both parents? What if you are selecting one set of grandparents over another? What if you want the ability to change to non-grandparents in the future as the grandparents get older, but don't want to hurt their feelings?

We feel really good about our decisions for now but also feel like these conversations could stir up a lot of relationship dynamics for a very unlikely event! Should we draft another document that outlines our wishes and hopes, or is less more?

We'd like your thoughts on the topic of legal guardianship for our two young children.

And you thought the politics of the guest list for your wedding were tricky! Seriously, I commend you and your husband for putting the time, thought, energy, and money into taking care of your wills. Too often young parents don't bother with their wills because they feel their assets are not significant enough to worry about, or they find it uncomfortable to have to think about something as unpleasant as their incapacitation or death, or they say, "What are the chances both my spouse and I die?"

This last point is valid. It is most likely you cannot think of one instance in your own life where both the parents died leaving behind young children. But as unlikely as this may be, you are wise to legally protect yourself (as with your medical directives) and your loved ones from outcomes which would not be to your liking, such as your children being raised by a sibling whose parenting philosophy is unacceptable to you.

Regarding your questions about legal guardianship for your two young children, I consulted with Robert L. King, (www. RobertLKing.net) a Fort Lauderdale attorney who specializes in wills and probate. Mr. King explains that probate is the court procedure to determine who receives your assets that are in your individual name when you die. It is "intestate" if you do not have a valid will and "testate" if you do. So you do not avoid probate since the will must be admitted as valid by the court.

In the unlikely event that both parents die and they have not left a will, the courts will take over and make important decisions on the parents' behalf, starting with a court-appointed guardian. However, by naming your guardian(s), you generally avoid the conflicts that can erupt between family members over who would be best for raising your offspring.

In your will you may list as many people as you want to be potential legal guardians for your children. The order in which you list them is important: In the sad event that your children need to be raised by their legal guardian, the courts will start at the top of your list and ask each in turn if they are willing to assume the responsibilities of raising your children. If the first one declines, the next party on your list is asked.

As you are drawing up your will, it is up to you whether you ask each person on your list if they would consider being a legal guardian, as there is nothing to prevent you from listing them without their permission. If you decide to get permission from your potential legal guardians to be listed, you don't have to tell them where they are on the list.

In this way, if you prefer one set of grandparents over another set, or one sibling over another, or one close friend over another, you can simply tell all parties that you would like their permission to name them as potential legal guardians. They will no doubt appreciate knowing that they are being listed along with others. They can either accept or decline as you are drawing up your wills, or at the time the list, alas, needs to get activated. In any event, they know you thought enough of them to name them as possible legal guardians for your children.

You and your lawyer can easily change the order of the list in the future, dropping some and adding others, as circumstances change. Factors such as illness, geographical moves, or different parenting philosophies may motivate you to reevaluate your list of legal guardians. People on the list at one time do not need to know they are no longer on your updated list or that the order of your list has changed.

Regarding the possibility of hurt feelings resulting from somene not being named or not being first on the list, Mr. King has advised young parents to write letters to the parties explaining why certain decisions have been made. These letters can be written by the young parents and left with the lawyer, to be shared only if both parents die and legal guardianship becomes an active issue, or they can be shared at the time they are written, or any time in between.

I want to close by giving you kudos for doing everything you possibly can do to ensure your children will be provided for and nurtured by people you have handpicked because their values best reflect what you want for your children in the unlikely event you and your spouse die. I hope all young parents will follow your example and take care of those wills they've been putting off. A well-considered will is a gift to your children.

{Chapter 37}

Our New Neighbors Are Annoying Us with Their Proselytizing

Dear Dr. Gramma Karen:

My husband, our two sons, ages seven and nine, and I live next door to my sister, her husband, and their seven-year-old daughter and ten-year-old son. We intentionally live near each other; we all get along really well and there is a lot of back and forth between our two houses.

A few weeks ago a new family moved into the house on the other side of my sister—we'll call them the Smiths. The Smiths have four children, ranging in age from 6 to 12. They seem like a nice family, but here is the situation: religion is very important to the Smiths. The problem is that everyone in the Smith family, even the younger kids, is constantly asking us why we don't go to church and why don't we join them in the weekly religious meetings they have in their home. One of the Smith kids has started telling our kids that all of us are going to hell, the devil will get us, and that they are praying for us.

My sister says we should ignore them when they start in and just thank them for praying for all of us. I disagree with my sister. I am finding the situation getting progressively more annoying and I think we should say something to them. What do you think?

You have a couple of options. One is to stifle your annoyance for a period of time and go your sister's route of just ignoring, or minimally acknowledging, the Smith's religious palaver. You may find over time that the Smith family is drawn more to other families who share their religion. They may just naturally drift away from your family and that of your sister's. After all, they are new to the neighborhood, and are understandably trying to get themselves established and build a sense of community.

If this option is not right for you, as close as you and your sister are, you may want to part company with her on how you deal with the Smith family. It sounds like your sister is okay with the Smiths proselytizing to her family, whereas you are not. If you decide you do not want the Smith family to discuss their religion when you and your family are around, I suggest you approach the Smith parents and say something along these lines: "You have expressed to us on several occasions that your religion is very important to you. However, you need to know that we consider religion to be a private and personal choice, and as such, we would appreciate it if you would not discuss your religion with us any more as it feels like pressure to become involved with your religion. This is not something we choose to do."

If the Smith family continues to bring up their religion, you can can simply repeat, "Your religion is a private and personal choice, so please do not discuss it any further with us." If you say this enough times, they should get the message. If they are unable or unwilling to respect your family's request, you would certainly be justified in curtailing or ending your interactions.

Whatever you decide to do, it is important that your children clearly understand the choices you and your husband have made regarding your own faith and religion, or lack thereof, e.g., staying with the faith your parents practiced when you were growing up, choosing a faith different from what your parents practiced, or not practicing any religion. Most important is that you address with your children any of the Smith's beliefs they've expressed that are not part of your belief system and are causing your children to feel threatened, frightened, or confused.

I close with this thought: There is a difference between someone who is genuinely and intellectually interested in understanding choices you've made, and someone who has taken you on as a project, needing you to accept choices they've made. In the former situation interactive and satisfying discussion can result. In the latter situation, there is little room for dialogue. There are times it is appropriate to make certain topics off limits for relationships to continue, and based on the feelings you've expressed, the Smiths proselytizing to you and your family is an example. Respect, tolerance, and acceptance needs to be a two-way street.

{Chapter 38}

My Granddaughter Wants a Cellphone, but Her Mom Says No

Dear Dr. Gramma Karen:

My granddaughter Becky will be ten next month. She told me she wants a cellphone for her birthday, but her mother said she's too young and can't get one. Becky said a lot of her friends have one and she doesn't see why she can't have one, too. She said she'd be willing to help pay for it. She asked me to talk with her mother about it. I never really thought about kids and cellphones, so at this point I don't have an opinion one way or the other.

I have a great relationship with my daughter Mari, so I felt very comfortable having this discussion with her at Becky's request. Mari said she just feels the kids grow up so fast today and she thinks ten is just too young to have a cellphone, but maybe when Becky is 12 or 13.

Mari and I both read your column and we'd be interested in whether you think a ten-year-old should be allowed to get a cellphone.

I can't tell you whether I think Becky should be allowed to get a cellphone because 10 year olds have different levels of maturity and responsibility, but I can give you some things to think about as you make your decision.

You may find some data on cellphone ownership and usage interesting, starting with the fact that 84 percent of all Americans own one. Granted, kids often exaggerate when they say, "Everyone else can do such and such," but in this case, statistics support Becky's comment that a lot of kids her age have their own cellphone. In a recent New York Times report, 36 percent of 10- and 11-year-old kids have cellphones, an 80 percent increase since 2005.

This same report describes the top five uses of the phone for this age group: (1) Call my parents (88 percent); (2) Call friends (68 percent); (3) Text messaging (56 percent); (4) Emergency purposes (54 percent); (5) Play games. A gender break down indicates that girls tend to use their phones to make calls and send messages, whereas boys are more apt to instant message and use the Internet to download games, music, and video.

Becky was born into a digital world. Her future productivity and success require her to be digitally savvy. In fact, three out of four parents think it is just as important for their kids to know how to use digital media as it is to learn traditional skills like reading and writing (Harris Interactive Poll, 2007). Becky is probably already computer literate; she perhaps has her own computer, or at least access to one in her home and/or school. The cellphone, like a computer, is just another digital tool, but when kids are in their own homes online, this can feel safer to parents who worry about these same kids using a cellphone responsibly when they are on their own.

Becky's mom wants to be assured that Becky will be a responsible cellphone user. (I smile as I recall reading about one mom who made her son, who was known for losing things, carry around a toy phone for a several months to prove he would not lose it. He was highly motivated and did not lose his toy phone.)

One suggestion I have for all parents to help lessen the anxiety about their kids having their own cellphone is to educate their kids with some guidelines for cellphone etiquette. For example, the parents can sit down with their child and a blank piece of paper. The parents can then ask the child his/her ideas on what the rules should be for being a responsible cellphone owner; the parents then add their suggestions to the list.

After discussing each one, the child or parent can write down the ones to be included, this document comprising a contract or agreement. The child signs the document, confirming that he/she agrees to the rules and commits to following them. This approach does not guarantee 100 percent compliance, but it can provide some appropriate awareness, education, and discussion. Below is a sample document I created; it may be copied and modified.

Then, once parents get the cellphone situation under control, they can gear up to deal with their child's request to upgrade to a smartphone (defined as a combination of a traditional Personal Digital Assistant or PDA and a cellular phone, although cellphone and smartphone technologies are quickly merging). Accurate numbers of kids owning smartphones are harder to determine, but one data set indicates that almost a third of the applications on smartphones owned by parents who allow their children to install applications were downloaded by their children. At what age do parents think a child should have his/her own smartphone? In a recent Crackberry survey, only 11 percent of parents felt 11 and 12 year olds should own a smartphone; 35 percent believe children 13 to 15 is the right age; 38 percent think 16 to 18; 13 percent think 18 or older is appropriate.

Back to whether Becky should get her own cellphone. In making a decision about whether to let a child have his/her own cellphone, I think a parent needs to consider the child's level of maturity, his/her history in being responsible, and I would add a third, the preparation the child has had in learning how to be a responsible cellphone owner. Your decision may factor in any family plans offered by your cellular service provider, as well as your financial situation. Some family plans will add a device at no charge whereas others charge. And finally, you may want Becky to assume some financial responsibility for having her own cellphone.

Guidelines for Being a Responsible Cellphone User:
Agreement between Child and Parent

I (child) agree that I will:

1. Give out my cellphone number only to people that you (my parents) have approved.
2. Answer calls and respond to calls only from people you've approved.
3. Follow all the rules set by my school for using cellphones.
4. Always put people first. I will not stop talking with someone to take a call, unless it's an emergency situation.
5. Not use my cellphone while walking down the street.
6. Turn off my cellphone at meal times, i.e., family meals, school cafeteria.
7. Turn off my cellphone wherever my phone ringing or my talking could be a distraction to others, e.g., in a movie theater, museum, concert, restaurant, subway, bus.
8. Keep my voice mails short. Further, I will give this

information when leaving a message: My name, why I'm calling, and what the next step should be. For example, "Hello, Adam. This is Jack. I'm calling to see if you want to bike ride together this afternoon. Call me before 3 p.m. if you want to ride today. Otherwise, I'll see you on the bus tomorrow."

9. Never use the camera on my cellphone to take a picture of anyone or anything that could be embarrassing or disrespectful to me or to others.

10. Make sure the content of my e-mails and text messages is never hurtful, disrespectful, or embarrassing to anyone.

11. Be the only one to use my cellphone. I will not share it with others.

12. Comply with the conditions of my cellphone contract, e.g., minutes and functions I am allowed to use.

Chapter 39

We Don't Want to Lie to Our Grandchildren about Santa Claus

Dear Dr. Gramma Karen:

We have two grandchildren, five-year-old Danny and three-year-old Jessie. We live near them and spend a lot of time with them. As we head into the holidays, we foresee a problem. Our daughter-in-law Bethany "does Santa" in a big way, e.g., leaving cookies and milk out for him, planting reindeer hooves marks in the yard, having the kids write him letters telling him how they've behaved, and what gifts they want.

This year we're anticipating that Danny, who is a questioning and thoughtful little boy, will be asking if Santa is real. His mother will say yes, Santa is real, and we know she expects us to say yes, too, when we're asked.

My husband and I think this idea of saying Santa is real is nonsensical and deceptive. We don't want to lie to Danny, but neither do we want to get ourselves into hot water with Bethany by not supporting her Santa lie. Our son tends to just go along with Bethany on these types of matters. Do you have any advice for us?

When young parents position Santa to their children, it comes down to picking one of three basic approaches: (1) They present Santa as real; (2) They present Santa as not real; (3) They present Santa in a specific context. Each approach represents a combination of a parent's personal experiences with Santa as a child and the values the parent is trying to teach the child. Let me provide some detail on each.

"Santa is real." Parents who present Santa as being real typically relate experiences from their own childhoods about the fun and magic of believing in Santa: the excitement of sitting on Santa's lap and talking with him; the anticipation of his arrival; the wonderment of his sleigh, elves, and reindeer. These parents do not view themselves as promoting a deception, but rather, they feel they are helping their child participate in an age-old cultural custom that is fun and enchanting.

In addition, they tend to believe it is not a traumatizing big deal when a child learns that Santa is a myth. As one parent starkly puts it: "Life is not a beautiful dream, but a chaotic mess. So let the kiddies have a few years of delusion before everything hits the fan for them. It can't hurt to ease them into reality." In short, these parents feel telling a young child that Santa is real is harmless fun.

"Santa is not real." One parent feels very strongly: "If you tell your kids Santa's real—you're lying! Also, it's creepy, the idea that you'd tell your kids a mysterious bearded stranger in a red suit is always watching them and judging them and that if they are good they will get toys. That's messed up." Another parent says, "I was raised being told the truth about Santa, as were plenty of other people. [When my mom was raised believing in Santa] . . . she says she remembers feeling she wasn't good enough to get gifts from Santa. They were very poor growing up."

Another parent said that he never quite trusted his parents

again for telling him Santa was real, not to mention that he felt stupid for buying into it in the first place. And finally, there are those children whose religion and/or ethnic culture precludes them from embracing Santa, leaving them often feeling different or ostracized (http://www.huffingtonpost.com/april-daniels-hussar/parenting-crisis-the-sant_b_397153.html).

For these parents, when asked if Santa is real, the straightforward answer is no. There is no deception, fabricating, winking, or crossing fingers involved. (Parents using this approach are often surprised and amused when their child insists Santa is real. So there!)

Putting Santa in a specific context. Parents who adhere to this approach often present Santa as part of a traditional story based on a real man (http://www.stnicholascenter.org/pages/around-the-world/) who has evolved through some wonderful imagination into Santa Claus, a fun holiday character with magical attributes. Children can still participate in the fun aspects of Santa and know it is part of their ongoing fantastical pretend play, yet not feel they have been deceived by their parents.

Taylor Newman, a blogger for *Parenting Magazine* writes: "I might just tell Kaspar (her two-year-old son) that Santa is a fun Christmas character, and that some children believe he's real, and that we can still hang our stockings while knowing Santa's part of a story. Kids easily walk the line between what's real and imaginary all the time. Perhaps allowing Kaspar the insight that what's magic about Christmas is that all people, young and old, love to imagine, will maintain the special parts of Christmas without requiring I uphold a farce . . . and without 'leaving him out', or prematurely jaded, as a result of my honesty" (http://www.parenting.com/blogs/parenting-post/so-about-santa-claus).

Another way to put Santa in context is to use a familiar and reliable old friend, *Sesame Street* (http://muppet.wikia.com/wiki/ Santa_Claus). This Web site contains over 60 different enactments and skits using real people and many of the Sesame Street characters dressed up as Santa. Viewing some of these together can help a child appreciate the pretend aspects of Santa while preserving some of the fun and enjoyment. For these parents, when asked if Santa is real, they might answer, "Santa Claus is a really fun holiday character, and here are some of the stories about him." Some children will themselves attribute realness to Santa, while other kids will hone in on the pretend and creative aspects.

I suspect this third approach, putting Santa in a specific context, is one that will work best for you and your husband because it does not involve what you consider to be deception, yet it doesn't leave you in the "Bah, humbug!" role of ruining the fun aspects of Santa for Danny and Jessie. In addition, hopefully it doesn't put you at odds with Bethany.

It seems important to Bethany that Santa play an active role in her family's holiday activities, so I suggest you share the three approaches I have outlined and discuss how this can be done in a way that you mutually honor each other's positions: Incorporating Santa into your family traditions (meeting Bethany's needs), but doing it in a way that lets you and your husband join in the fun without feeling you are being untruthful with your grandchildren.

{ Readers' Comments }

Dear Readers,

"We Don't Want to Lie to Our Grandchildren about Santa Claus" generated a lot of interest. Several readers said it doesn't really matter what the grandparents think, should their grandson raise the Santa Claus question because, as expressed by one reader: *"The question poses a bigger problem than the issue of whether or not Santa is real. As a grandparent, I do not think we have the right to undercut a decision made by a parent unless it endangers the child. I do not think that there is any endangerment here. To ask the question is to assume that a grandparent has the right to overrule a parent's decision. No can do."*

Other readers disagree that the parents' position should prevail. They feel the emphasis should be on trying to find a balance: *"Hopefully those grandparents will take your advice and stay true to themselves (while honoring the mother's wishes) and they will all be able to enjoy what the holiday is really about, that is, having fun, being kind and spreading joy! I don't like to rock the boat . . . I just want everyone to get along. I think you giving them a way to help celebrate the holiday with fun characters is great for everyone! I don't think it needs to be so deep."*

Another reader finds balance by differentiating between direct and indirect lies: *"I am someone who does not like to lie to children. I try to keep things real, even in scary situations—always letting kids know the truth within context. I hate the whole Santa thing. However, I have three little kids and Santa is part of this world that we live in. So I have decided to talk about the 'magic of Santa'—a recommendation from my mom. This way I feel like it is not a direct lie, and it somehow goes along with the spirit of the season that the 'magic of Santa' allows him to be in many places (all over the world) at once."* Other readers also said they liked the idea of talking about the enchantment and magic of Santa because children can enjoy the stories and myths in their younger years and yet not feel they have been lied to when they get older.

This comment from a young mom succinctly summarizes

the issues and their implications: *"This was a very thought-provoking piece for me that made me consider a whole range of things, including stories about religion. It made me think about what I will say in the next couple of years as my kids get older and are able to question the Santa Claus tale. I don't want to perpetuate a big deception, but I do love the fun and make-believe.*

"This year, with a two-and-a half-year-old and a ten-month-old, we are sticking to the traditional script, but I have to admit that much of it is for my own benefit! I have a lot of fun talking about the magical side of the holidays and I know my daughter enjoys it, too. But I don't think she'd enjoy it less if I tempered the content a little bit more, especially as she gets older. Because she's only two, she also thinks that Olivia (the pig) is real and is her friend who might come over to play some day. It's tough to burst bubbles, and I don't always like to, but I can make sure I'm not deliberately inflating them too... I really appreciate your suggested third approach—it's nice to know it's not all or nothing!"

And to the reader who wants to know how to handle the Tooth Fairy or the Easter Bunny, I suggest the same three choices to address them as the ones I presented for positioning Santa Claus: (1) They are real; (2) They are not real; (3) They are magical characters and there are lots of fun stories about them. One story that can be a truly fun experience for the entire family is to watch the animated movie *Rise of the Guardians*, the story about an evil spirit, Pitch, who tries to take over the world, but must first defeat a combined force comprising, Santa Claus, Jack Frost, Tooth Fairy, Easter Bunny, and various other delightful characters. Believers, non-believers, and agnostics of all ages can enjoy this movie without challenging or spoiling anything for anyone else.

{Chapter 40}

Grandparents and Grandchildren
Make Us Smile

Dear Readers,

The following was sent to me by one of my readers who found it on www.guy-sports.com.

I like the idea of using humor for my final chapter. I hope it makes you smile!

Message on Grandparents' Answering Machine

Good morning . . . At present we are not at home, but please leave your message after you hear the beep.

beeeeeppp . . .

If you are one of our children, dial 1 and then select the option from 1 to 5 in order of your "arrival" in the family so we know who it is.

If you need us to stay with the children, press 2.

If you want to borrow the car, press 3.

If you want us to do your laundry, press 4.

If you want the grandchildren to sleep here tonight, press 5.

If you want us to pick up the kids at school, press 6.

If you want us to prepare a meal for Sunday or to have it delivered to your home, press 7.

If you want to come to eat here, press 8.

If you need money, press 9.

If you are going to invite us to dinner, or take us to the theater, start talking: We are listening!

What Is a Grandparent?

(Taken from papers written by a class of six-year-olds.)

Grandparents are a lady and a man who have no little children of their own. They like other people's.

A grandfather is a man, & a grandmother is a lady.

Grandparents don't have to do anything except be there when we come to see them. They are so old they shouldn't play hard or run.

It is good if they drive us to the shops and give us money.

When they take us for walks, they slow down past things like pretty leaves and caterpillars.

They show us and talk to us about the colors of the flowers and also why we shouldn't step on 'cracks.'

They don't say, "Hurry up."

Usually grandmothers are fat but not too fat to tie your shoes.

They wear glasses and funny underwear.

They can take their teeth and gums out.

They have to answer questions like "Why isn't God married?" and "How come dogs chase cats?"

When they read to us, they don't skip. They don't mind if we ask for the same story over again.

Everybody should try to have a grandmother, especially if you don't have television because they are the only grownups who like to spend time with us.

Grandparents don't have to be smart.

They know we should have a snack time before bed time, and they say prayers with us and kiss us even when we've acted bad.

Grandpa is the smartest man on Earth! He teaches me good things, but I don't get to see him enough to get as smart as him.

A six-year-old boy was asked where his grandma lived. "Oh," he said, "she lives at the airport, and when we want her, we just go get her. Then when we're done having her visit, we take her back to the airport."

{Acknowledgments}

I'm glad I listened when you urged me to write this book: Jezra Kaye, Adelaide Lancaster, Herb Ouida, Gary Rancourt, and David Rottman.

Mommybites.com co-founders Laura Deustch and Heather Ouida (my wonderful daughter!), I cannot thank you enough. You said, "Do it!" and supported my idea for an advice column. I also thank my former Mommybites.com editor Elise Jones, and my current editor Jennifer Rojas, for editing my columns and making sure they are posted on time.

To the following I thank you for the many ways you've supported and promoted Ask Dr. Gramma Karen: Tara Campbell, Ellen Franks, Anya Garcia, Jezra Kaye, Sheila Kreiger, Adelaide Lancaster, Janet Logozzo, Mary O'Connor, Andrea Ouida, Amy Morik, Peter Rancourt, Sheila Rancourt, Renee Sullivan, Bonnie Waldron, and Deb Zeigler.

A special thank you and a big bear hug to Herb Ouida, my "bellwether reader," for your prompt and thoughtful comments to every column I've ever written.

Tons of appreciation and barrels of affection to Jordan Ouida—you make being a mother-in-law so easy!

I love that you call me Gramma Karen: Aidan, Alex, Andrew F., Andrew M., Antonus, Ashley, Ava C., Ava K., Caroline, CG, Casey, Christopher, Clair, Curran, Devon, Ellie, Gabrielle, Hailey, Isabella, Jaime, Jeffry, Jesse, Justin Me, Justin Mo, Kyle, Kylie, Layla, Maddie, Magnolia, Matthew, Mikey, Nicholas G., Nicholas

O., Nolan, Olivia, Ori, Perri, Ryan Me, Ryan Mo, Sloane, Suta, Tanner, and Teague. I hope the list keeps growing.

A grateful and loud shout-out to the best two executives with whom I have ever worked—for modeling all the right stuff about management, leadership, communication, and building relationships: Colonel Harvey R. Greenberg (retired), U.S. Air Force; David L. Rottman (retired), Managing Director, Career Development Group, JPMorgan Chase & Co., and the author of *The Career As a Path to the Soul.* You were great teachers and mentors and will always be treasured friends.

Much love and gratitude to my husband Gary, my thought partner and first editor for everything I write. You always ask the right "What about . . . ?" questions. Even though I often stubbornly push back, you're always spot-on.

I want to give a special acknowledgment to Diane O'Connell, my developmental and production editor, for her solid advice and expert guidance. It is a pleasure to work with you!

Finally, I thank: all my Ask Dr. Gramma Karen readers; the parents, grandparents, and other family members who place their trust in me when they seek my advice; those who send me their comments and experiences to be shared.

We're in this together. It's all about the kids.